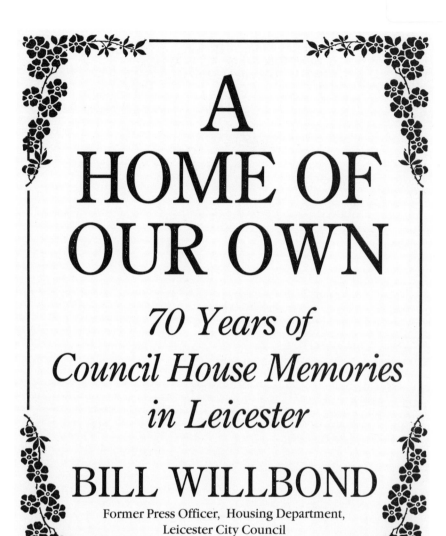

A HOME OF OUR OWN

70 Years of Council House Memories in Leicester

BILL WILLBOND

Former Press Officer, Housing Department,
Leicester City Council

Leicester City Council

PUBLISHED BY LEICESTER CITY COUNCIL

Leicester City Council, Housing Department,
New Walk Centre, Welford Place,
Leicester LE1 6ZG

**THE RIGHT WORSHIPFUL THE
LORD MAYOR OF LEICESTER**

LORD MAYOR'S PARLOUR
TOWN HALL
LEICESTER LE1 9BG
TELEPHONE: (0533) 526060

As we go through life, it is difficult to realise that we are part of the process which makes history. The story of Municipal Housing is part of the fabric of life in our City; we are fortunate that Mr Willbond has taken the trouble to record some of the human stories before time has overtaken them and they are lost for ever.

Decent housing for all our citizens is a goal we must all seek to achieve. We in Leicester owe a debt of gratitude to our forbears who took the first steps, from which we now enjoy the benefit.

I hope Mr Willbond's book achieves the success it deserves and I wish it well.

Councillor Peter Kimberlin
The Right Worshipful the Lord Mayor of Leicester

Contents

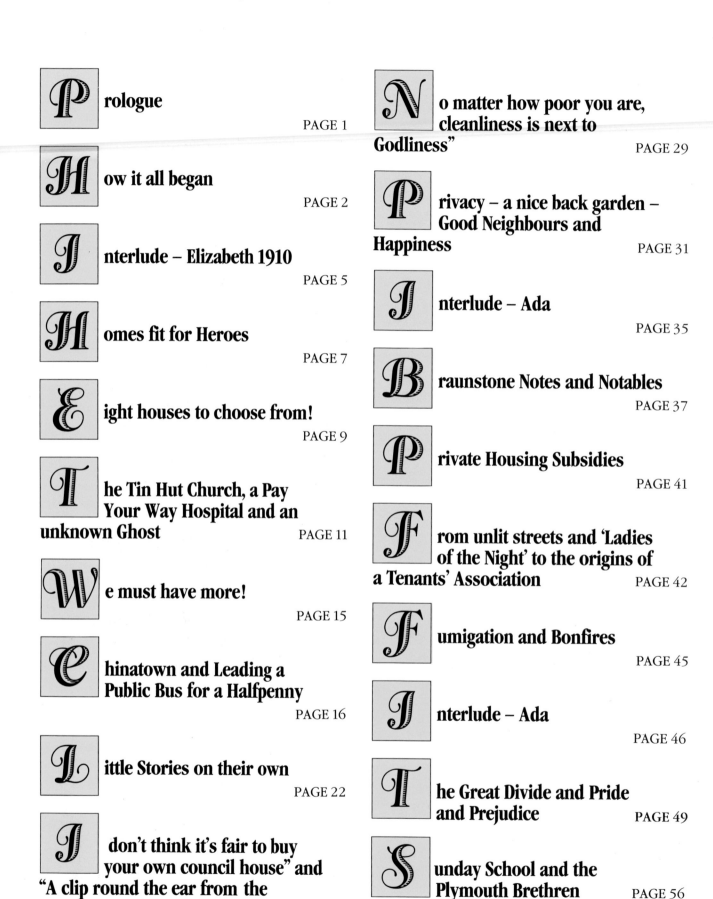

I know a little street,
Where old friends meet,
I'd like to wander back
Some day.

To you it may seem old
And oh so tumbledown,
To me it means a lot,
It's my home town.

I may be rich or poor,
But still I'm sure,
I'll be welcome as
The flowers in May.

I know a little street,
Where old friends meet.
And treat you in
The same old way.

Favourite song round the pub piano

Preface

'A HOME OF OUR OWN' is all about Leicester City's Council estates and the people who live on them.

Published to coincide with the City Council's 70 years of housing celebrations, the sketch does not in any way attempt to be a detailed social history of Leicester council housing. This has been done, in depth, by many people over the years, including Ned Newitt with his essay 'From Slums to Semis', which will be available later in the year and can be recommended to the serious student. In contrast, 'A Home of Our Own' first looks briefly at living conditions in the 19th Century and the need for Council houses. It then recounts the personal memories of tenants, and looks at estate development through their eyes. It gives a glimpse of what their living conditions were like before estates were built and their early lives as tenants; how their estates developed in the thirties, and how they built a community spirit that was to see them through the war years and beyond. And that spirit has come through in many diverse ways. For example, a building built entirely with community skills; community anger when the Council dared to allow a dual carriageway to cut their estate in half, and a whole street providing crockery for a wedding!

During interviews with tenants, many stories were told; some funny, some sad. Unfortunately, space does not allow all the stories to be related. However, as many as possible have been included, like, for example, 'The Sunday Pub' and 'The Day the Mulberry Harbour turned up in Leicester'.

There was something else that came out strongly, too, particularly with the older tenants, and that was pride. Pride in their homes and gardens; pride in their estate and pride in the heritage which they had helped to create. But many expressed fear. Fear that through the seeming indifference of the younger generation, that heritage would decline; and fear that if their estates were ever totally privatised, unaffordable rents would mean that heritage being lost forever. And there's the paradox.

So to all those people who invited me into their homes, I say thank you, and thank you for your memories too. Memories which truly make this sketch, your sketch.

Thanks are also due to the staff of the Humanities Section of the Reference Library, Bishop Street, for their help and guidance with my research; the Leicester Mercury for free use of photographs and permission to use extracts from their newspapers; Councillor George Billington for reading my draft; Jane for unscrambling my interview tapes; all those friends, former colleagues and Councillors who gave me such helpful advice, and finally, a special thank you to the Director of Housing, Ted Cantle, without whose assistance this sketch would still be an idea.

Bill

Bill Willbond

Dingy! Dirty! Damp! A little street, but the houses are home. In these surroundings, neighbourliness reigned and a Spirit was born...

Prologue – 1858

When Jimmy came to Leicester in 1858, it was a very different place to the Leicester we know today.

Jimmy had left the poverty of his home in Ireland to seek work in a prosperous English town. And prosperous it must be, for wasn't it true that with all the new industrial developments, factories were going up all over the place, providing work for everybody? Of course it wasn't strictly true — at least the work for everybody part. Some towns, in spite of the industrial revolution as it were, still had an unemployment rate of over one man in thirty. With a wife and two children, and another 'on the way', Jimmy knew he had to take a risk and emigrate. To stay in Ireland would be to face abject poverty and handouts. So what was best; to see his family on the brink of starvation, or go where he could at least earn some money and provide his family with a home? The decision wasn't hard, for among other things, Jimmy was a proud man. And so it was, that not long afterwards, he found himself in Leicester town on a warm day in May - one of the many Irish immigrants looking to Leicester for a better way of life.

The Irish, who lived in a tight community in St. Margarets Parish, were a mixed lot - in fact, as mixed a lot as you could find anywhere in the world. And because of this very mix of overcrowding and terrible living conditions plus the Irish 'reputation', they were soon all, rightly or wrongly, labelled as trouble makers - strangely enough, a situation that was to repeat itself some 70 years later in a totally different environment in West Leicester.

It was hot for early May, when Jimmy and Mary together with 10 year old Liza and 9 year old Emma, moved into a one up, one down in a dingy, 15 house court off Belgrave Gate.

Standing in the shabby little room, Jimmy looked round at the peeling dirty brown walls; the damp patches; the rusting grate whose cold ash was mixed with the corpses of cockroaches and other nameless creatures, together with a rat, and wondered what on earth he had done. Even the few sticks of furniture he had managed to buy didn't alter his depressing view. It was hot. Stifling hot.

No air seemed to be getting through into the house, the only indication of movement being the smell of the court.

Outside in the dusty courtyard with its ash pit, single tap and stinking communal lavatory, the girls were exploring. Next door on the step of No. 5 sat a young girl about Emma's age dressed in a not too clean pinafore. She wore no shoes or stockings and was staring down at the dark, dirty ground, tears leaving white runs on her grubby face. Inside the house voices were being raised, and a baby was crying. "Hello" said Liza.

In the dirty room she now had to call home, Mary sat on one of the rickety chairs wondering when her child would be born. Next door, the raised voices ended with a woman's cry of pain...

A court dating from the early 1800s - prior to dustbins, ashpits were the order of the day

How it all began...

"Water came mainly from communal wells, inevitably polluted by raw sewage..."

BEFORE the Municipal Corporations Act of 1835 (and for some time afterwards), Leicester was a town of narrow streets and dingy houses, mostly crowded together in the low lying parts of the town. The houses were, in the main, 'one up, one downs', set in filthy, putrescent courts, often flooded after rain because of their aspect.

In those days, there was no sewage system, refuse disposal or water on tap as we know these today. The emptying of stinking cesspools and the dumping of throat-gagging rubbish, accumulated over the months, was the responsibility of the householders.

Water came mainly from communal wells, inevitably polluted by raw sewage from the cesspits and effluent from the river, particularly after rain. It's no wonder,

therefore, that deadly illnesses were rife and that 'summer fever,' aided by the hot, airless conditions of the homes, carried off many good people.

With the advent of democratic elections - the direct result of the Municipal Corporations Act - Leicester finally had a body of Councillors 'good and true', who set about righting the awful living conditions of the populace. Headed by such 'Fathers' of the town as John Biggs, they lost no time in tackling the great problems of waste disposal, water supply and the improvement of health.

It is not within the scope of this sketch to go down the avenue of all Corporation reforms, therefore, let it be sufficient to say that the developing Corporation began to lay the foundations of Leicester as we know it today.

In the field of housing, Leicester fared better than most, mainly through plentiful building land, a caring - if yet, still weak

Backs of houses in Lower Grove Street showing the luxury of three lavatories to eight homes!

2

Corporation, and a zealous Medical Officer of Health tackling the problems of overcrowding, lack of sanitation and the resulting diseases.

From 1860 onwards, the town's population began to increase rapidly as immigrant workers from depressed towns came to seek employment in the developing boot and shoe, hosiery and knitwear industries. But this immigration immediately raised a problem: how were they to be housed?

In 1861, the population stood at 68,000 with, statistically, 4.7 persons per household. Ten years later with a population of 95,000, the household statistic was virtually the same; without doubt a testimony to the 'industry' of those entrepreneurs who, in ten short years, had laid new roads and built some 5,000 houses to go with them.

West End. Hinckley Road. Narborough Road. Highfields. Belgrave Road. In the 60's and 70's, building spread in all directions, mostly upwards to healthier areas. Unfortunately in spite of (or because of) their 'industry', the builders didn't pay too much attention to the byelaws and the requirements of the Corporation. In the 1840's, Leicester contained none of the

A typical court in Lower Brown Street. This was still inhabited well into the 20th Century

3

*Sandacre Street:
a communal tap
and a gutter
down the middle
of the street,
communal
toilets (on the far
right of the
picture) and gas
light*

4

airless, almost windowless back to backs common in other towns. Yet by 1864, records show that some 1,500 had already been built and that over a third of these would still be occupied 70 and 80 years later!

At the turn of the Century, with fresh running water, sewage farms, fever and isolation hospitals and more control over housing, Leicester was on its way to becoming one of the more prosperous of the industrial towns.

In the decade leading up to the beginning of the War, Leicester suffered a trade recession and many people were

unemployed. This of course affected their ability to pay rents and many were letting out or sub-letting their own front rooms. But with the advent of War, unemployment disappeared; but so did thousands of able bodied men.

By the outbreak of the First World War, Leicester was a totally changed place from that in 1835. Railway stations. A gas department. Electric lighting and an electric tram system all added to the town's prosperity. Housing continued to develop - the majority of the property being rented, at rates varying between four shillings and seven and sixpence per week.

Interlude – Elizabeth 1910

Elsie and Jim

As Elizabeth Merry watched Ada, one of her several grandchildren cleaning around the house, she thought it was time she went and saw her own mother.

Hadn't seen her for ages and her conscience was pricking her. Liza, her mum, lived in a one-up, one-down in a Britannia Street court, surrounded by the trappings of the early 19th Century. The house was next door to Rolleston Lodging House. A grand place. Charged fourpence or so for a night's lodging, but well worth it. Nice and clean it was. None of your riff-raff there - even if a man did have to pin down his boots with the legs of the bedstead! Looking at it, the court didn't seem much different to the days when Elizabeth lived there. But at least, they now had running water - even if it was one tap to the court - and with sewers laid, the smell wasn't anything like it used to be. She remembered as a little girl she used to relate it with the stink of the court where Grandma lived. Thinking of grandma, she harked back to the day, nearly twenty-three years ago and nine children earlier, when she had married Tom. Gran and grandpa had been there together with Emma and Tom's family. They had celebrated in the Woodboy Inn, just across the Court from Liza's. A nice place. That made her think of Amos Sherriff who had lived there. How was he these days, she wondered. She hadn't seen him for ages and ages. He was a serious chap though. Interested in politics. Elizabeth didn't know then, but Amos was not only to be a leading light in the Local Labour Party; be associated with hunger marches, and fight for his class; he was, in time, to become Mayor of Leicester!

Elizabeth wished her Grandpa was still alive. She remembered most his Irish accent - soft and lilting. But, then, he always was a soft spoken man. What a pity he had died of summer fever.

As she thought of summer fever, Elizabeth absent mindedly fingered the five vaccination marks on her arm. Big they were. Large as pennies and shiny. You could still see the scratch marks where the doctor had made her arm bleed as he scratched in the cowpox. Cowpox! No wonder her husband Tom had been angry. She had been made to have the vaccination by law. Something to do with the Medical Officer of Health, or something. Anyway, it was

Tom and Elizabeth Merry, surrounded by some of their family outside the 'workshop' on Junction Road.

Hughes shop on the corner of Woodboy Street and Russell Square in 1926 – where the author bought his first pair of long trousers!

supposed to prevent summer fever and other things.

Elizabeth smiled to herself as she thought of Tom's attitude when the doctor came around to do the vaccinations. She could see him now. Standing there stony faced, as the doctor vaccinated the family. As soon as the doctor had gone, Tom was across the room to her in two strides. He seized her arm and began to suck and spit furiously as if sucking venom from a snake bite. He wasn't going to have his wife full of pus from a cow! It hadn't made much difference though, she still had the scars to prove it!

When Grandma Mary McGee had died last year, her Aunt Emma had moved to London to stay with her widowed sister-in-law.

Amos Sherriff, a leading local politician

Elizabeth wondered if she would ever see her again.

Elizabeth came back to the present. This wouldn't do, Tom would be home soon - by but he was a grand shoemaker! Elsie would be home soon, too. Elsie was her youngest. Bright as a button. She'll make something of herself one day.

Elizabeth wondered if Tom had made his mind up, yet, about moving into Junction Road. It was a nice house they had the chance of. There was a big front room with a shop window and it would be ideal for him to sell his shoes from. There was also room for a nice little workshop at the back. It would be nice for the kids too. If only Tom wouldn't drink so much, she thought. Elizabeth sat up as she heard Elsie coming in from school. School! Elizabeth didn't let on that she couldn't write. She could read a little, and she could talk. But for her that was enough. She really had had no time for learning, she reflected, for when she was four years younger than Elsie was now, she was already working 'in the shoes'.

"Homes fit for Heroes"

FTER the First World War, councils all over the country were to be faced with a very testing time.

By 1919, the slogan: 'Homes Fit For Heroes' - that good intentioned promise to the survivors of the Somme, Ypres, Flanders and other blood baths, was finally coming home to roost.

After four years of war, new houses were virtually non-existent. With the pre-war building force of skilled men now sadly depleted; with building materials for homes very hard to come by - partially through priority being given to industrial building - the private builder, who up to now had been the sole provider of housing stock, found it beyond his capabilities to cope with the situation. Also, people were demanding something new in housing. No longer were they going to put up with the 'cottages' built for a previous generation, they wanted something better; more amenities; more space! They were fed up with four years of purgatory and misery of war. They wanted the better and happier life that they had been promised. They demanded it. And such was the clamour, that in 1919, Parliament finally passed an Act making Local Government responsible for providing 'Homes Fit For Heroes'. Thus Council Housing was born.

Of course, it wasn't as cut and dried as all that. There were many strings and requirements attached - as one might expect with any Government legislation, not least restrictions on what could and what could not be done, and what could and what could not be spent (does anything really change?), but for the purposes of this story, let's say that Council housing has arrived.

If the Act of 1919 was a Pontius Pilate one, it was also a challenge to which many councils had difficulty in rising. Never before had they been faced with the problem of providing housing for the populace. But Leicester was to be the exception that proved the rule. Exception, because in Leicester, subsidised Council homes for people who could not afford to pay current rents had been proposed as early as 1888 by Councillor John Richardson, a somewhat radical Tory.

In 1897, the Estates Committee submitted a plan to build a block of flats in Winifred Street with proposed rents of between 2/3d and 9/- per week as against the 6/- to 10/- per week charged by private landlords. But when the first block of flats was occupied in 1900, the rent had increased to between 3/- and 5/- per week. This was due, in the main, to higher building costs brought about by alterations to the original plans. Alterations made and insisted upon by the Local Government Board. But at least, the flats had been built and were occupied by grateful tenants.

And so it was that 19 years on, and with experience of both house building and dealing with the vagaries of Government Departments, an enterprising and enthusiastic Housing Committee was formed. Not put off by high costs, it proceeded to erect houses on Coleman

"...they wanted something better..."

7

Leicester's first council housing in Winifred Street. First occupied in the 1900s as 'artisans' dwellings', they were modernised in 1966 when this picture was taken. They are still in use today

FACING PAGE: Houses built on Coleman Road in 1920/21 in a revived 18th century architectural style. The formal pediment, symmetrical windows and the generous overhang of the eaves all reflect great attention to detail

Road, Narborough Road and Gaddesby Avenue. In all, only 746 houses were allowed to be erected under the Act, and with thousands of applications already received, it was obvious that a housing shortage had begun. For the occupants of new council homes, it was almost Heaven on earth - even if they did have a few difficulties!

Eight houses to choose from!

ET Mrs. Annie Smith, now in her 90's, and one of the original tenants on Coleman Road, take up the story.

"I got married after the war, and my husband and I moved into rooms in Baggrave Street, off Green Lane Road, next door to my mum. I found this very handy, of course, but I didn't get on with the other people there, and when our son was born we decided to have a go for a council house.

"Well I kept going to the 'Housing' - I never missed a week. Then, one day in 1921, I met a woman who had a home in Deepdale.

"We got talking about council housing and she said 'Have you got a house yet?'. I said no. So she said 'How long have you had your name down?'. When I told her, she said 'Well, I've only had mine down for three months and I got my house straightaway!'. Well, that did it!

"I went straight up to Housing, and told them. But as soon as I mentioned Deepdale, the Housing man said: 'You don't want to believe all you hear from that quarter, your turn will come'.

"It did, two years later! Finally, I had had a house offered.

"When I told my husband, he said we should get the key and go and look at it first. So me, being silly, I went to Housing and asked for the key so we could go and have a look. And the chap in Housing said: 'All the time I have been in Housing, no one has asked to see the place first!'. And, do you know, he then gave us eight individual houses to choose from! There were three on

> *"...my husband put his foot in the door of number 148 and said: 'This is it'."*

Even in the '50s, unmade roads were common on the Coleman Estate, such as this one between Coleman Road and the Goodwood Estate

10

Wayne Way. Three on Deepdale and two here - 148 and 150. We looked at them all and my husband put his foot in the door of number 148 and said 'This is it'! and that's how we came to live in Coleman Road.

"After Baggrave Street it was wonderful. Three bedrooms upstairs, three rooms downstairs and a bath and toilet - the Council modernised the house three years ago and put me a toilet upstairs and installed central heating. It's lovely. I have been very happy here."

Annie talked on about unmade roads and broken pram springs. Of St. Chad's Church which was then nothing more than a tin hut (of which more later). And how in some roads on the estate the Council seemed to let anybody in!. But I am jumping the story...

The Tin Hut Church,
a Pay Your Way Hospital and an unknown Ghost

 GEORGE Audley was just five years old when he moved with his parents into a new council house on the Coleman Estate. The house was on Langhill and he recalls quite clearly the day they moved in.

"We moved from a terraced house in Baggrave Street with our few bits of furniture piled up on uncle Joe Audley's cart. Uncle Joe was a carrier who lived just round the corner on Bridge Road and on the morning he came round with his horse and cart and we loaded up. Mum, Dad and I walked alongside - just like a funeral procession, and after what to me seemed hours, the new home hove in sight. Oh! What an eye opener it was! Electric lights. A bathroom. Bedrooms with fireplaces. Copper in the kitchen. A toilet and coal-place near the back door and, in the living room, a coal fire range (which I used to have to black lead every week) with an oven one side and a water tank on the other. And there was a garden too."

Mr Audley's father had been gassed during the war and suffered from asthma. And when his father was really ill, they found the bedroom fire a god-send. With a fire to warm the room and a bronchial kettle filling the room with moisture, his father was made as comfortable as possible. "That was", George remarked, "if we had the coal!"

George's other memory is of the kitchen floor which was rough concrete and had to be scrubbed every week. He said, "Over the years, the concrete rose in the middle and

eventually had to be flattened. But they didn't tile it. They just left it rough concrete again, no doubt eventually to rise yet again in the middle."

George then talked about St Chad's. "St Chad's started as a tin hut". He continued: "It had been used by the army during the war in France, but when the war was over - and because there was a shortage of buildings, lots of huts were returned to England. And St Chad's 'Church' was one of them. It was in use both as a church and community building until a new brick church was built, eventually to be replaced by the modern church you see today on the corner of Coleman Road.

"In those days, we used to make our own entertainment..."

TOP: The interior of the "Tin Hut" Church

BOTTOM: St Chad's, the 'Tin Hut' church, as George would have seen it – orginally a hut used by the army in France in 1914 – 1918 War

11

"As a kid, I used to love the street traders. There were two vegetable and provision men who used to come round twice a week with their horses and carts. (There were no shops on the estate, only a post office and a wooden hut on Clumber Road corner, where we used to fetch our newspapers from). One was named Smith and the other had a call or cry which sounded like 'Jeremiah'. Of course that wasn't his name but to us kids he was always 'Jeremiah' - he didn't look biblical though!

"In those days we used to have to make our own entertainment. We used to play with 'fag cards'. These we got from the men who smoked, and when we had them in complete sets - 'Butterflies of the World', or 'Famous Cricketers', or whatever, we used to play two games. In the first you held a cigarette card up against the wall and let it drop to the floor. Then the next lad came along and did the same. And as soon as one fag card dropped on top of the other, or covered part of the other, then all those that were on the floor were yours. Then there was 'skimmers'. One card was leaned against the wall and you used to skim the others at it. If you were succesful in knocking it down, then, again, all the cards, on the floor, were yours. Marbles was popular as was snobs. You could buy snobs from the shop, but as most of us couldn't afford them we used to make them by tying shoe buttons into bunches.

"'Weak 'Osses' was a game of strength. One lad (the Pillar) would stand with his back to the wall then the remainder of his side would bend forward head to tail, the first one pressing his head firmly into the 'pillar's' stomach. Then the opposing side would take a long run and leap-frog, the object being to land as near to the first person's neck as possible. After this the remainder of the team would jump and hope like mad that when the third, fourth or even perhaps fifth person landed on the poor unfortunates the 'oss would collapse! Another game was called 'Graters'. I don't remember much about the rules but we used to have to roll a ball down the gutter in such a way that it stopped in the grate. 'Pitch and Toss' was played with a piece of wood and of course we used to play war games. There was lots of old equipment lying around from the 1914/18 war - helmets, webbing and so on and of course we kids always used to dress up and relive the war. I remember it was always an argument who was going to be the Germans!"

Mr Audley's father used to work for the Corporation and used to pay so much a week to cover his family for hospital treatment and dispensary.

"The nearest hospital to us was the City General and to get there we always had to walk quite a long way. There were no direct roads as there are today, the only indication of the site of the hospital being the pepper pot chimney which has now been demolished. Nothing was free, and all beds were sponsored. Payment was by ability - plus of course the cover my father used to obtain for us. It was almost like a means test when they tried to assess how much money you had got. I know my father, out of his wages, used to pay one and sixpence a week to cover hospitalisation at the City General. I remember visiting grandmother once and it was awful. The beds were all crowded together, in fact so close you had a job to get between them. And when you went to see the doctor and he gave you a prescription then, of course, you had to go to the dispensary and pay for it.

"In the summer we used to go to Evington to camp for the day at 'Piggy's Hollow' which is just behind St Deny's church. To get there we used to have to go along Cut Throat Lane. This was a road that went towards Evington from Coleman Road. It was called Cut Throat Lane because a foul murder was supposed to have been committed there, when a relative of the local butcher had his throat cut".

Mr Audley left Langhill in 1941 and his memories are all happy ones.

Oh! The Unknown Ghost. It is said that to be in the vicinity of what was Cut Throat Lane on a certain night, gives one a feeling of unease, especially if you are near the old spinney and the original mortuary where the murder was supposed to have been committed. Even the street lights will not disperse this feeling. It is, of course, pure speculation, but could the oppressive feeling be due to the presence of a murdered man?

CITY OF LEICESTER
HOUSING & TOWN PLANNING COMMITTEE
PARK ESTATE HOUSING SCHEME
LAYOUT PLAN
(PRELIMINARY)

We must have more!

IN 1923, another Act of Parliament enabled the Corporation to build a further 638 houses. However, it was fast becoming clear that the Housing Committee would need to think big. Up to now, they had built a few houses here, a few houses there. But with a waiting list of 5,700 applications in 1924, small was no longer beautiful. Houses would have to be erected quickly and economically in large numbers. With this urgency in mind, by 1925, the Council had obtained a large tract of land on the south side of the town, Saffron Lane, Park Estate. They also acquired Braunstone.

Because of difficulty in obtaining suitable building materials in the quantity required for rapid building of the houses, plus the shortage of a skilled workforce, the Council decided to erect 1,500 concrete houses on Saffron Lane using the Boot and Pier method of construction - houses that 65 years later would become the centre of an ongoing housing controversy.

Bearing in mind that a sameness of house building on such a scale could possibly lead to a new suburb becoming an eyesore a few years hence, the Council went to great lengths to make sure the estate was well planned. Straight streets were out. Instead, planning followed the natural contours of the land and four different designs of house were erected. Some with parlour, some without, with rents reflecting the accommodation. Thus tenants could choose according to their means and requirements.

To make for even more interest, houses were built with different roofing materials. Some would have grey roofs, some red and others a restful shade of green. In the case of Boot houses, texture and colour was the order of the day, the rough cast exterior ranging between yellow gravel, white limestone and grey granite. Add to this, a variation in chimney stacks, casement windows and sash windows; and here was a pattern which hundreds of other houses on other estates could follow. And so the Council proceeded to build.

But what of the new tenants: the people who were to transform Saffron from an 'interesting estate' into a living entity.

Chinatown
and Leading a Public Bus for a Halfpenny

"...it took about 6 weeks for the stove to come..."

IC Bright was brought up on Saffron Estate in the 20's and 30's. Vic was only 18 months old when, with his father and mother Doris and brother Phillip aged 5 months, he moved into 10 Belton Close.

I first spoke to Mrs Doris Bright who is 86 years old and asked her how she felt about moving into Belton Close from Bonchurch Street.

She said: "When I first moved into Belton Close, I thought it was heaven, because for 3 years we had lived in 2 rooms. We left Bonchurch Street to move to Belton Close when the children were quite small Phillip

5 months and Victor 18 months. As I said before, Belton Close was like moving into paradise, because we had a bath and the children could have a separate bedroom. What I couldn't get over was the fact that I didn't have to go very far, other than to a tap in the house to get water. In Bonchurch Street we used to have to walk through the house and fetch water from the next door neighbour's tap.

"We had little furniture, but my husband had a good job at the time and we were soon able to furnish the house as we wanted. The children went to school in The Newry which was built on an old pond, and later

they went to Linwood Lane'. I asked Mrs Bright about the community when they first moved into Saffron and if there was any community spirit. She continued: 'Well of course when we moved in we knew nobody, and we had been there nearly a fortnight before I spoke to a next-door neighbour. She came to ask me if my stove had arrived. I said no and we had to cook on a fire. It took about 6 weeks for the stove to come. That was the first time I had spoken to anyone but, of course, afterwards, as we got to know everyone else, naturally a community spirit developed". She continued: "The house was in lovely brick - not concrete, and what was really fascinating was that you could actually fill the coal-place with coal and not just have to have it in half cwts. as we did in Bonchurch Street". She added: "Do you know, I can't tell you just what it was like living in two rooms. Only those that have lived in two rooms can really know what I'm talking about".

At this point Vic Bright came into the conversation. "Yes," he said, "when we were kids we all called Saffron 'Chinatown'. You see, there was such a mixture of nationalities - all types and such different personalities. There were characters with horses and carts, wheelbarrows, and there

Heaven on earth. Saffron in the 30s

Just a few years
later and there
were children's
playgrounds
such as this one
on Barfoot Road
and Littlegarth

18

was an old fruit and veg man who used to come round shouting for, amongst other things, votes. I well remember him touting for Councillor Mawby - and that's a long time ago!

"As kids we had great fun. Where we lived, there was a jitty between Southfields Drive and Belton Close and at the bottom end there was an off licence which was owned by Charlie Cave. He had several sons and a daughter, and we always used to think of them as 'rich'. Charlie used to leave his back gate open - presumably for his children to go in, and because we kids had no money, we saw nothing wrong in taking a few bottles out of the back yard and taking them into the shop to get a penny back on them.

"On a Sunday morning, the jitty became virtually an outdoor pub. Because the nearest pub was on Saffron Lane and the next nearest in Wigston, Charlie Cave's off licence became a gathering point on Sunday morning - and weekdays for that matter - for

the men of the estate. We kids used to think it was great. We used to sit at the back of our six foot high fence at the bottom of the garden listening to the men telling jokes and playing cards. And I am sure I learnt all about pitch and toss with coins, and heads and tails and odds, long before a normal boy should.

"What they used to do, of course, was buy all their drinks in the off licence and take them in to the jitty and drink. I suppose between house and house the jitty was probably 100 yards long and 9 feet wide, so it was a nice gathering point. When the men had all gone home, they left all the bottles on the path and we kids used to go and pick them up and take them all back to the off licence and get more pennies. I suppose that was one profitable way of keeping the estate clean! We didn't have much entertainment in those days, perhaps the best was when, with mum and dad and my brother, we used to go to the Aylestone Cinema. I well remember seeing Al Jolson in The Singing Fool - but then, my dad was crackers on Al Jolson!

"We had some sporting characters on the estate too. Norman Plummer, Leicester City's Captain in the 48/49 cup final, lived down the road from us and I also had the pleasure of meeting Joe Muskett, a wonderful footballer who taught Norman the tricks of the game.

"Another highlight of the week was on a Friday when we kids used to go and meet dad out of work and he would take us to somewhere like Woolworths in town to buy a penny soldier or even a tupenny soldier, and then it was back home.

"Another thing I remember was how proud people on the estate were of their gardens. Very few people had nasty gardens. My father used to grow flowers and I well remember him talking with other members of the estate about the wonderful carnations he had grown. Another famous institution was the Great Universal Club. Mum used to pay sixpence a week and I remember we got our three-piece suite that way. But of course, there was no shame in this. We were very proud. Our house was spotless and we certainly had nothing to be ashamed of.

"School, too, was pretty strict. I well remember Mr Halford the headmaster. Even though I was head boy he didn't spare the cane and very often thrashed me. But it didn't do me any harm. I also remember lovely rock apples.

"Norman Plummer's mum, in her old fashioned black overall, used to sell them from the house. She'd make the rock apples in the washing boiler in the back kitchen and we used to buy them for a halfpenny. But, of course, if they had got coconut on them, it cost a penny! I know that one day, the toffee apples got me six of the best, because, by the time I had got back to school, having eaten my apple on the way, the gates were closed; and not to be there on time was a mortal sin. But we were used to people being strict. My father was strict as I think most of the fathers were on the estate. There was none of the casual attitudes you get from kids today. We always used to say 'Good morning sir', or 'Good morning mister'; we used to run errands for people and didn't get paid for them, because we didn't expect to be paid. It's something I think was born in us. But of course we didn't do it all for love. I used to collect coal on a Saturday for people from Saffron Lane. I used to bring a 1/4 cwt. for ½ d. but that's not a lot, really. I know when I was about 9 or 10 I often used to carry a cwt. of coal and still only get paid a halfpenny. Apart from coal, I used to go shopping for people, and I well remember one particular old lady

Carts and prams in the queue to collect 28 lb bags of coke outside Aylestone Gas Works

who used to give me a list about 10 inches long. But even when the shopping filled two bags, it still didn't cost more than 9/-! Then, the other money earner was when it was foggy and I became a Corporation bus director! I only wish I could have been a real Director in those days but my job was to stand in front of the bus when it was very very foggy with a torch in my hand to guide the bus along. For this I was paid the odd halfpenny or penny. But with all the odd jobs I did I used to think I was a millionaire!

"A regular summer pastime for us kids was to go a walk along the Path Fields. We used to get a bottle of water and a few sandwiches and off we'd go. We went down towards what you now call the Pork Pie Library just inside Wigston Lane, turn left and there was a road which led to the fields. I don't know why they were called the Path Fields, all I know is that people used to say 'Are you going to the Path Fields today?' It was a lovely walk. There was a grass airfield nearby that used to have aeroplanes come and give rides. I remember one pilot called Rod McKay, and my mother, being a bit of

a daredevil, had a ride in his plane for 7/-. Very expensive, but she thought it was marvellous.

"I would imagine scrumping is something that still goes on with the present generation in the right place, but in my day it was a serious business.

"Just beyond the Path Fields you came to the Rolleston Estate where there were some lovely apple and pear trees. Snag was, if the gamekeeper saw you he would literally shoot at you. I remember the man quite clearly. His name was Walker and as a kid I can still remember looking up and seeing the hairs coming out of his ears and nose. He chased me many a time. But one day there was a bang behind us and Ted Lankey my friend went home crying because he got buck shot in his backside. Of course we didn't go to the police because we didn't want any trouble. So we all kept quiet until the Monday morning. Then the teacher brought a man in who said: 'These boys have been in the fields and they have been scrumping my apples'. The headmaster said that if those of us that had been scrumping

Roadworks on Saffron Lane outside the "Pork Pie Library", Spring time 1953

didn't step forward, everyone in the school would be caned. Believe it or not, it's the honest truth, all nine of us stepped forward. Perhaps there's a moral there somewhere!

"But I didn't just go scrumping on the Rolleston Estate. I well remember Sir Stanhope Rolleston and Lady Rolleston and very often I would go to the house and clean their grate. It was a massive thing and for cleaning this with black lead and then cleaning Sir Stanhope's boots, I used to get 2 shillings a week.

"I used to try and time my work so that when I came out I could catch Cocky. That was the name we called Mr Cocks the milkman with his float, his churn and his white pony. He used to give me a lift the length of Saffron Lane and drop me at the bottom and then I'd run like a cat out of hell to get to school.

"I know that your environment as a boy or girl tends to shape your future. Mine was certainly shaped by the estate. It was just so clean and nice when compared with slum areas like Wharf Street. Flowered gardens, lawns, clean roads, discipline at home and school and a strong community spirit. These plus a happy-go-lucky childhood are what I am sure shapes your life for the future. Maybe it was the flowers and the greenery that eventually made me become a florist and owning my own business. At least, that's what I like to think!"

Milk was delivered door to door from churns carried on horse-drawn milk floats.

21

Little Stories on their own

THE following letters were sent in to the Council by various tenants and former tenants, and are included not just because they were sent through the post but because in their own way they sum up Council people and Council Estates.

From Don Connolly,
Chair, New Parks Tenants' Association:

"The incident that I refer to took place on New Parks during the rent strike 1972/1973.

"We were checking on tenants who had promised to join with us in a protest at the high rents being demanded at the time.

"Whilst he was upstairs in the loft trying to mend the valve, the woman's husband came home and my friend had to beat a hurried retreat. I still remember him being chased up the street protesting he only wanted to fix the plumbing and the chap saying 'I'll fix your plumbing if I catch you!'".

From Mrs Simpson, Queniborough:

"I heard your request for information about the early Council House Estates on Radio Leicester this past week and thought I may be able to help you. There's not much I can tell you but you are welcome to this if it is of any use to you.

"My old friend had knocked on a door and was reassured that the occupant would indeed support us. She also said that she had a problem with an upstairs ball-valve, asking my friend to repair it for her. I must explain that my friend was one of nature's gentlemen and would do anything to help anyone. He was also pure of mind!

"My father returned disabled from the First World War and when he married he had to share someone else's house for the first four years of my life and we were among the first to move into the Saffron Lane Estate, which must have been about 1926. We went to Bloomfield Road and I think the house was number 40.

"I was, at this time, a rather sickly child with chronic bronchitis and rickets, which must have developed through lack of sunshine, etc. I remember being shown the trains running along at the bottom of the garden through the bathroom window and my parents so excited about moving into a new house after what they had had to endure before.

"I always seemed to be playing in our garden, or someone else's with their children, so neighbours must have played an important part in our lives. And I must have got gradually stronger and stronger, because I developed a love of the countryside which I have never lost. In fact if I have to live in town for any reason now, I can't be happy.

"There were a few shops on the Saffron Lane. The only one that I can remember was the lovely chocolate shop which had all sorts of tempting sweets and chocolates. When I was old enough I used to run all the way to do the shopping, which seemed a long way then, but there was always a small bar of chocolate for going.

"I went to the primary school, which I think was in the Wigston Fields area; long walks again. We left Bloomfield Road when I was 10 and I didn't enjoy that. But luckily we moved back to Windley Road on the same estate and were there for a few years. I used to play and walk in the little park that was opposite the house so that I could be seen by my mother. Later we moved to Southfields Drive and I attended Linwood Lane School. I enjoyed my time there and left when I reached 14 years of age".

From Mrs Barbara Cavanagh,
Crown Hills Rise:

"I heard the broadcast on Radio Leicester about your Housing 70 Years.

"My late parents moved into 315 Green Lane Road as soon as it was built - I was born there. Perhaps the following may help you.

"There were two large bedrooms and a small one - just a box room really. In the two bedrooms there were fireplaces and when it was very cold mother would light a fire. The bathroom was smallish - cast iron bath and a wash hand basin. The coldwater tank was in the bathroom. It was a very cold room - no sun ever warmed it and there was no heating until later in life when we had a power plug installed on the landing and we were able to have an electric fire in there (very dangerous).

"For a number of years the electric meter was on the landing, so high up the meter reader had to borrow a chair to stand on so that he could read it!

A coal-fired copper and hand-pump in the kitchen provided hot water: "…Sometimes it was a job to get the fire going on Mondays – wash day."

23

The large yellow
'stone' Belfast
Sink in the
corner of the
kitchen

24

"Downstairs, the pantry was near the front door. It was quite large with a stone floor. Three shelves were along one wall and onto another wall. The window was half glass and the other half was in mesh. This let all the dust in so we pinned two thicknesses of gauze over it.

"The front room was only used on special days - no-one could afford to keep it warm all the time.

"In the kitchen was a large copper. Sometimes it was a job to get the fire going on Mondays - wash day. The sink was a large yellow, shallow one. After the war a new modern sink was put in. I remember it was put so high my mother could not reach it and it had to be lowered, also the draining board slanted the wrong way and the water ran down to the wall instead of into the sink! The kitchen walls were not plastered, just bricks painted green at the bottom half and yellow at the top.

"The living room was quite large really. Until well after the last war we had what was known as a 'fish & chip' range. The fire had two doors that could be closed to 'draw' the fire up. The heat went all around the oven. On the top were three holes with lids on, we could remove these lids and place saucepans on them so a whole meal could be cooked at the same time. That, of course, if the wind blew in the right direction! One Christmas our goose would not cook in time so we ended up with corned beef and had the goose in the evening!

"The floor in the living room was made of square red tiles - they looked lovely after they had been scrubbed, but what a job! Later on we had a carpet square on the floor and life was a lot easier and warmer.

"The front room floor was wooden and the kitchen was rough concrete. Stones soon wore holes in the mats. The hot water tank was in the living room - heated by the fire - and the hot water pipes were fastened to a board on the walls for all to see (and the dust to collect on).

"We had a small garden at the front of the house. A standard rose tree stood in the centre. At the start of the year snowdrops poked their heads through the snow.

Crocuses followed and in the spring daffodils and tulips grew among a carpet of bluebells. We had a large garden at the back which supplied our vegetables (organic grown of course!). To reach this we crossed a slabbed yard. Next to the back gates stood the toilet and the coal place. When it snowed a path had to be dug before reaching the toilet. Despite lagging the pipes and having a paraffin lamp, also a sack covering the top of the door, we still had quite a few burst pipes as the winters were very cold then. Imagine, too, how quick we had to run if we had tummy trouble!

"None of the tenants had much money, but when dad came home with his wages the first thing that was put away was the rent. Money for food came second and alongside was the money for gas and electric.

"Monday was wash-day. On a fine day all the neighbours had their clothes blowing in the wind. To save money, mother and her neighbours shared the starch - taking it in turns to make it. Over the year this saved quite a lot of money.

"After my dad died, we asked mother if she wanted to move to a smaller place, but she would not and stayed there until she died in 1975.

"I understand these houses have been modernised but to us they were little palaces - after all we did have a bathroom and lots of people did not.

"I hope this has been a little help to you. I have written to save you the journey, also this is written as I remembered".

In the 1920s a mangle, tub and dolly made the housewife's chores a little easier on wash day

25

From Mrs Ford of Helmsley Road, Saffron Lane Estate:

"My husband moved into this house in 1923. He was captain of St. Christopher's Boys Brigade and he also served in the First World War.

"After he lost his first wife, I married him and moved into the above address in 1946.

"There were always two buses for the estate. I remember hearing the cows mooing on Shackerdale before houses were built, and a narrow bridge very difficult to cross due to traffic.

"My house had a pump in the kitchen, and water had to be pumped up to the bathroom to get a bath. I still have an old fashioned copper in the kitchen where on wash-days 40 years ago, a fire had to be lit and washing boiled on that day. The house had old fashioned narrow paned windows but I certainly like the new ones they have

been replaced with. Apart from that, very little has been done to modernise the house - I would like a storm door for example to keep out the cold, rain and snow etc. from the porch.

"My husband had a lovely garden, growing beautiful fruit and vegetables etc. In those days pride came first. Steps were scrubbed etc. But on looking around now, sadly, all this is neglected - especially with the young tenants. Yes the olden days were best. The house has no central heating and is damp and cold in winter but I like it and do not wish to leave. Memories to me are living things but I look back and thank God for a good husband; good marriage; God first in our lives and the result: happiness. It used to be Aylestone Park Estate; I wish it was called that now instead of Saffron Lane!"

"I don't think it's fair
to buy your own council house" and "A clip round the ear
from the Community Bobby"

ITTING in the warm front room of his house on Netherhall Estate, Mr Gould recalled his family's beginnings.

"My mother and father started life together in a two-up, two-down cottage in Bath Lane, with fifteen people sharing the communal yard toilet. Conditions were unbelievable; conditions that eventually brought my sister down with diphtheria.

Dad was serving in the Royal Navy at the time and I think this, together with my sister's ill health, helped us to get a Council house in 1920.

"The house was one of sixteen or seventeen in a semi-circle encompassing Dunton Street, Central Road and Repton Street. To mum and dad, after the cottage in Bath Lane, it was a palace - running water; a bathroom; and a toilet and coal-place

"I remember once, three of us had been scrumping..."

Typical court cottage, showing the common yard and communal toilet shared by two households

27

attached to the house. Mind you, it was still cold in the toilet and with being lead piping, the water often froze in the winter. But we eventually countered that by heat from an oil lamp. The only thing was we had gas light instead of electric. But that didn't really matter and it was one of my jobs to go and fetch the replacement mantles.

"The area was nice too. There was grass all about us and we used to swim in the River Soar - it was so clean and clear. Then they came and built hosiery factories and that cut us off from the river. It also meant that we lost our 'Green'. It was just like a village green and a policeman used to graze his donkey on it.

"Talking of policemen, our community one was great. He was good fun - and fair. But if you got a bit out of line, then you got a good clip over the ear and he would report you to your dad!

"I remember once, three of us had been scrumping, and we had stuck the apples up our jumpers. We were sitting on an iron seat at the top of the green when our policeman came along. 'Hello lads, where have you been then?' He got the usual reply: 'Nowhere!' 'I see, move up then and let me sit down and whilst I light my pipe tell me what you've got stuck up your jumpers'. We did, and he made us eat every single one. Then he went and saw my dad. They were great days but the discipline didn't do any harm.

"I enjoyed school. I first went to Mantle Road but later was transferred to Balfour Street. There, we had a plot of land which we could dig and plant - smashing. Eventually, I went to King Richards Road Intermediate School.

"Going back to the house, it had one big room with a sort of annexe at the bottom. A larder, pantry, three bedrooms and a bathroom. We had some wonderful times there. After I left, mother stayed on for a few years but eventually we got her moved into a bungalow.

"I joined the Navy, and when I came out in 1947 decided to buy my own house. But I saw some friends in the building trade and they said 'No way! without savings you don't stand a chance'. So I put our names down on the waiting list at the Housing Department. In due course we had children and finally got our Council house. It's a lovely house; I think we're very lucky. Of course I would like to buy it but I don't think it would be fair. You see we were glad of this house and, when we die, someone else will benefit as we did."

"No matter how poor you are, cleanliness is next to Godliness"

MRS. Wooley was born in Belton Close in the 30s and it is interesting to compare her memories with those of Vic Bright who lived but a few doors away. The first real memory she has is of neighbourliness.

"Everyone was always friendly and helpful. Say for example anyone died then the neighbours would always hold a collection." Mrs. Wooley went to school in Southfields Drive and afterwards to The Newry. She remembers vividly bonfire nights. She recalled: "Every bonfire night, we always used to build a big fire in the middle of the road - we were allowed to do that in those days. And when the fire was going, folk used to bring along potatoes and onions to roast in the embers. It was lovely. And if you had got any old furniture or anything you wanted to get rid of, it used to go on the bonfire - well it did save the Council from collecting it didn't it! Because we were poor, we had to make our own entertainment. We used to play a lot of games like rounders and hide and seek,

which, when it was foggy, was lovely! Then there was whip and top. Of course, it didn't matter too much playing in the streets those days because there was hardly any traffic about, not like there is today. Then, it was mostly horses and carts with traders like the breadman, coalman and milkman. I remember my mother always used to leave the pantry window open when she went to work, so that the milkman could lift it up and ladle the milk into a jug on the pantry shelf. Of course you could do things like that in those days because you could trust people - not like today.

"I have already said we were poor and I know Mum worried about keeping four children, but she always used to say: 'However poor you are, cleanliness is next to Godliness.' And this was quite true because, although we hadn't a lot of furniture, the house was spotless - and so were we. But then that's how they were in those days and maybe it was this that made people respect other people's property.

"The gardens were important to us, too. We had quite a big one and everyone mucked in working on it and particularly keeping the weeds down. We didn't think it fair that seeds should drift into neighbours' gardens. And that seemed to be common to the area, because everyone's garden always seemed neat and tidy and there was never any rubbish lying about.

"When I was 17 my mum died and I know the Council were very concerned about my welfare. In fact, their concern is something I shall always appreciate. But I had a brother

ABOVE: "Pussycat, pussycat, where have you been?"

LEFT: Keeping weeds down – "We didn't think it fair that seeds should drift into neighbours' gardens"

Abbey Park, Leicester.

The Pavillion in
Abbey Park as
Mrs Wooley
would remember
it.
It was destroyed
by fire in 1959

30

and elder sister who was married and they looked after me. Really, it was a case then of all working together. One of my chores was to do the shopping along Southfields Drive and it was there with rationing and everything else that I learnt to hate queueing and I still hate it today. It was quite a good shopping row though, because there was Worthingtons', the Co-op, a fishmongers', a grocers' and greengrocers', a chemist and a fish and chip shop. On my way home I used to have to pass the off-licence on the corner of the jitty and I remember the men standing outside drinking beer. I was petrified - in fact I used to run all the way home!

"Talking of shopping takes me back again to when I was younger. Everyone was neighbourly, as I think I said earlier, but if by any chance you couldn't get out, then your neighbour would say, 'I'm going down to the shops - let me do your shopping for you.' Or they would invite you in for a cup of tea or coffee and a natter. But then, that was the attitude everyone had in those days. I know one of the things I really used to look forward to was the bus trips. Someone down the bottom of the road would organise a bus trip to Skegness or Yarmouth or somewhere like that for the day. All the families in the street would pay either weekly or, if they could afford it, in one lump sum and off we would go - the whole street! It was those sort of things that brought you close together. I suppose you could say Belton Close was a close-knit close! And it seems to me that those day trips really made people's holidays because you never heard anyone saying that they were going away for the week.

"Occasionally we would go in to town and that was certainly a trip. I remember one day, I was supposed to stay behind and wash the pots but I went with a friend of mine into town and we went to Abbey Park. And to me that seemed oh, a long, long way. And of course I was late coming back and my mum really told me off. She had been so worried. But parents then were really concerned for their children. They had compassion and the children's welfare at heart - always.

"I stayed at Belton Close until I was 25 when I left there to get married. They were certainly happy days."

Privacy – a nice back garden –
Good Neighbours and Happiness

RS. Clara Utting is 89 years old and living in Auburn House, Aikman Avenue.

She was married in 1921 at St. Saviour's Church and immediately put her name down for a Council house. She was asked where she wished to live and she said "I would like Coleman Road Estate, but they told me there was a big waiting list. And because I had no children I would probably have to have children before I could get a house anyway. So I moved into two rooms with my husband.

"In 1927 I gave birth to my little boy and went along to the Housing and I was told I could have a home immediately if I would have one on Saffron Lane. They were just completing the last few houses and I could certainly have one of those. So I jumped at it. I didn't care where I was going to live, provided it was a house. They asked me if I'd got the money for the rent. 'Yes', I said, 'I've got that put away' ('cos I was always careful, you know). My husband didn't get much money 'cos he was often out of work. You see, he had come out of the forces from World War I and work wasn't that easy to come by for the likes of him.

"I'll never forget going to the Housing that day. Frank, my lad, was just about three weeks old and my next door neighbour said 'Come on, I'll help you with the baby on the tram!' Well, like I said, I was offered the house, and the very next day, I got a letter confirming the offer. So that was it. I was in the new house at the end of that blooming week. After all, living in rooms we hadn't got much furniture to take anyway!

"No. 17 Cottagers' Close was a non-parlour type house. When I went to look at it, I said to the workmen who were finishing it off, 'Oh! Isn't it lovely. I'll feel really well off here.'

"My husband was working out of town at the time, and when he came home I said: 'Guess what, I've been up to the Housing and we've got a house!'

"So, we moved in and did the house up as much as we could. And what a difference to my old place! There, I had two tiny rooms, one up one down, a coal fire and nowhere to put the coal. And now, here I was, for 10/- a week with a three bedroomed house and most certainly somewhere to put

"Someone down the bottom of the road would organise a bus trip to Skegness..."

Clara's lad outside No. 17

31

Mrs Utting's Rent Card. 9/7d (that's about 48p) for a three-bedroomed house – not bad!

the coal - and, IT WAS CHEAPER! Of course, there were fireplaces in the bedrooms and when the little boy was ill it was nice to have a fire to keep the bedroom warm - if you'd got any coal that was! In those days we were very hard up - in fact everyone was hard up. I know come washday, I hadn't even got a mangle - but you had to add to the home bit by bit then. But we'd got a long washing line and I used to hang out the washing; squeeze it as much as I could, then let the wind take over and blow it dry. It used to be lovely, it had!

"Cottagers' Close had a big green in front of the houses. There were no homes across the other side, and where Stonesby Avenue is now, was just fields. There were just two shops at the crossroads and we used to go there for groceries. For everything else, we had to go into town. But you couldn't always go with little children. Mind you, at one of the shops you could buy almost anything - at a price.

"I remember Eyres Monsell being built. We would go there for a walk across the fields. Take the kiddies and go via the Black Pad. About four of us used to go - all neighbours. We'd just sit in the sun and let the kiddies run around. Then, sometimes for a change, we'd take them to Aylestone Park. We always got on together; we were all good friends.

"1936, Coronation Year, we went to all the neighbours and between us organised a street party for the kids (and us) it was lovely. The same with Christmas and New Year. On New Year's Eve we would all come out of the houses into the street and everyone would sing 'Auld Lang Syne' together - that was neighbourliness!

"It was the same after World War II. We strung lights in the trees and organised a party. My son put up loud speakers and it was great. We had music and played silly games. I know for one of them, all the women had to blow up a balloon till it burst. My husband said to me 'Don't let on, but I am going to let Mrs Godling win this one.' Well, she was a bit of a gal, you know! So he touched her balloon with his cigarette.

"I was at Cottagers' Close for sixty years - in fact, I had my diamond wedding up there. We took all the family out to celebrate.

"Going back to the time when money was tight, the one thing I always made sure of was the rent. Even if we'd got no food in the house, the rent wasn't touched. It was paid religiously, without fail. And of course, in

"Cottager's Close had a big green in front of the houses"

those days, you didn't get any handouts - not like today! But, you see I was born in Victoria's day when you really found it hard to survive, but somehow did.

"I went to work in Coventry on munitions when I was fifteen. Of course, you had to be sixteen really, but with not much work about elsewhere, there was no choice. Officially, you had to be sixteen years old and have an insurance card. But I went to the post office; told them I was sixteen and that was that. There were a lot of us girls went to Coventry from Leicester. We used to have to be there at 6.00 in the morning and would go on a special workers' train. You can imagine what time I had to get up. I once had to walk back from Coventry. I was on the night shift when a zeppelin came over. They put all the lights out and said: 'We daren't put the lights back on so you better go home'. So I did. I walked!

"Speaking of war, in World War II every tenant had to build an air-raid shelter in the garden. I know my husband made ours really nice. And every time the sirens went, down the shelter we would go. That is, except my husband. His duty was fire watching. Sometimes he would be up all night. But he still had to go to work the next morning.

"One of the things I can't understand today is the young ones' attitude to gardening. Some do it, but they're so different to my day. My husband used to keep our garden lovely. A nice lawn; vegetables at the bottom; flowers and a little greenhouse to grow tomatoes. But when young people moved in next door, they let the garden go. And soon, there we were, digging out someone else's twitch!"

Mrs Utting then told about Council house upkeep. "Even before the War" she said, "Officials used to come round and check on the house to see if you were keeping it in good repair. I remember once, they made my husband take a rambler out, even though it was only staked: they would not risk you knocking a nail into the wall. But when the Council modernised, that was funny. First they put some lovely railings around the house. Then they put a new roof on and insulated the loft. Then they took out the little windows and put some big ones in which we thought were lovely. Finally they took out the copper and replaced it with an electric boiler. Smashing! but when I wanted them to change the bath it was 'Oh No. It's too good!' So I let the matter drop. But then after we had been in the house sixty years I asked them again but they said 'Oh! no. It's too good!"

In conclusion, Mrs Utting said that perhaps the nicest memories she has of those early days was a house of your own with privacy and a nice back garden; good neighbours and, allowing for all circumstances, happiness.

Sadly she added: "But of course as the old ones died off and the young people moved in, the whole atmosphere changed. Everything was rowdy and noisy; and really, it was this change that made me finally leave".

Interlude – Ada

Ada, now eighty-seven, and living in a nice Council semi with her daugher and son-in-law, remembers the old days well.

"I used to clean the house for grandma Merry when they lived in Dundonald Road. Nice house. Front room. Back room. Kitchen. Three bedrooms and a private yard. But with her family, she needed it.

"Eventually, they left Dundonald Road and moved to Junction Road, where grandad opened his shop. He was so different from the shop and certainly Dundonald Road.

Elsie and Jim were still at home, and I suppose they must have shared a room. Aunt Nell lived next door - she had married one of the Rollestons from the lodging house, you know. And a salvationist lived opposite. Always used to be singing hymns. Then Elsie, she would be about twenty then, opened up a Milliners and Dress Shop in the shop next to grandad's old one. Did well, too. And of course

Ada today, happy in her council semi

Outside the Junction Road 'shop'

"By the time grandmother died, we were all married and so was Elsie. She had closed down the Milliners and she and her husband had taken a pub in Dover Street. Grandad was still alive, of course, and he went to live with them at the pub. Bet he enjoyed that!"

Brothers and sisters - Jim is on the right hand end of the back row

was a good craftsman and his business flourished. People would come from all over to have their shoes made and repaired. Trouble was, he liked a drink. And you can soon lose business that way. Still, his sons helped.

"Just before the start of the World War (Tom and Jim went to war and Tom never came back), grandad's business had fallen right off and he and my grandmother moved into a two-up, two-down in a four house Court opposite. It

that relieved the pressure on Jim.

"Going back to grandmother, I still used to clean up for her and I know I black-leaded her old range until it shone. Funny about that old range. When grandmother died, my sister and I sat up with Elsie. And in the night, all the cockroaches and things came out of the range, and my sister and me, we did nothing but keep sweeping them back into the hearth.

Braunstone Notes and Notables

BY 1925 the Corporation had built houses on Coleman Road, Narborough Road, Saffron Lane, Knighton Fields, Gwendolen Road and Uppingham Road. As we have already seen, of these, the Saffron Estate was the first large site to be developed, and its success convinced the Housing Committee of the advantages of developing large sites.

In October 1925, the Corporation purchased 1,200 acres of land including the pleasant parkland of Braunstone Hall - about 170 acres in extent, which, together with the house, 'would be maintained for all time as a public park'.

The Hall was the residence of Major R N Winstanley who was very reluctant indeed to sell the estate to the Corporation.

The episode of the Braunstone purchase is beautifully illustrated by Robert Guy Waddington in his 'Leicester, The Making of a Modern City'. Being contemporary to the period, and because one chapter explains fully the intentions of the Corporation, it is well worth quoting the relevant part verbatim.

"On the west side of the town, just over the border, was the delightful old world village of Braunstone, separated from the City by a belt of parkland and meadow, the whole of which belonged to Major R N Winstanley.

"It had long been near enough to the centre of the City to attract the attention of speculative builders who, it is generally reported, had made many attempts to pursuade the Major to allow them to develop some of his estate. He, however, resisted their blandishments. Other villages in the neighbourhood had either come into

"On the west side of town... was the delightful old world village of Braunstone"

FACING PAGE: A developing Braunstone moves away from the grime of the city.

Picture postcard village – Braunstone in about 1894

37

the City or the City had gone out to them, spilling its bungalows, its villas and even its factories over their fair fields: Braunstone with its meadows, its mansion, its park and its pool (a pleasant stretch of water), alone remained rural.

"The citizens on the west side of the town have reason to be grateful to the Major for keeping his estate intact for so long. It enabled them to take, without effort, an evening or Sunday afternoon walk, which would carry them, within a few minutes away from the bustle and noiseful populous industrial City. It was obvious, though, that sooner or later Braunstone would have to go the way of Humberstone, Belgrave, Knighton and the rest of the Parishes on the outskirts. Leicester must have room to grow and Major Winstanley himself must long have realised that he could not continue to push it (The Boundary) back. Probably it was the thought that if he was condemned

by Leicester's necessity, to sacrifice his fair fields to the builder, it was best that the builder should be one who would not make an eyesore of them; that influenced him to accept the Corporation's offer to take his entire estate off his hands. If his beloved Braunstone must be sacrificed, and it was clear that it eventually must, better far that it should be turned into a pleasant garden suburb than that speculative builders should chop it up and lay it out on a purely commercial basis.

"A sale was at any rate effected and the Leicester Corporation became owner of a magnificent estate of 1,200 acres. It is magnificent not only in size, but in possibilities. In the first place it furnishes the Housing Committee with sufficient land to meet any housing demand which is likely to arise within the next few decades. Thousands of houses have been, or are in process of being, erected upon it, and there is room for thousands more. It matters not that only 235 acres of the estate are within the City boundaries: the rest is within easy reach of the Clock Tower, Leicester's Centre, and the time cannot be far distant, when Braunstone will become administratively, as well as geographically, a part of the town. An important feature of the Braunstone purchase is that the Winstanley Park, with its Georgian Hall, comes within the estate, and thus that side of the town will have one of the finest open spaces in the Midlands, for it is intended to preserve it for the use of the public in its natural state. It consists of 170 acres, spacious enough to allow the three earliest Leicester Parks to be dumped upon it, if this were possible. The estate also permits of much land to be set aside for recreation grounds, playing fields, allotments, gardens and similar purposes.

"The estate has been very pleasantly planned. Through it will run the 'ring road' which is the feature of the Town Planning Scheme adopted by the Corporation some years ago. It is to be 120 feet wide and to provide easy communication between all of Leicester's suburbs, by providing a 'throughway' to link up the radial roads and enable the motorists to make their journeys without crowding the principal City streets and roads. Other roads on the estate will be 60 feet wide, while those used by residents only are to have a width of 40 feet. The houses along them, however, will be set back so that from house to house across the road, there will be a width of 70 feet. Thus, narrow streets will not mean lack of air space - better to give the individual tenants the benefit of the width than to throw it uselessly into the thoroughfare.

The Winstanley Oak in North Braunstone, so called because it was planted as an a acorn by Major Winstanley's daughter. It is now retained by planners as a historical feature

39

"It may be well to set forth the aims which the Leicester Housing Committee have wisely had in all their schemes for providing their tenants with homes. First and foremost they have insisted on erections which will admit the maximum of sunlight to every dwelling. In pursuance of this policy they have permitted no back projections to the houses they erect. Every cottage has a front garden and also a good stretch at the back for cultivation. It also has a roomy pantry or larder, well ventilated and facing away from the sun. No rooms open directly from the street, however small a cottage. Instead there is a wide entrance floor on the ground floor and well lighted landing above. The cooking and cleansing arrangements are all arranged for in the scullery, leaving the living room free for family and social use; and every dwelling has its bathroom with a separate lavatory basin.

"The only serious criticism that has been made of the operation of the Leicester Housing Committee's work, is that it has not provided good new dwellings for the very poor. The rents it is necessary to charge, low as they are in relation to the cost of building, are still too high for the very poorest. The Committee has now in hand other schemes for accommodating those of its citizens whose means are the most restricted, and if it is a success in this direction as it has been in its larger housing schemes, it will have done well. Its new houses in the suburbs have already released some of the smaller cottages in the centre of the City for the use of those who can afford nothing better; but many of these dwellings are not really habitable, according to present day notions of what a dwelling should provide, and it is hoped that within the next few years, the cottages which are now the slums of the City, and also those which are in process of becoming slums, will have disappeared, giving place to the superior dwellings which the Corporation will be able to furnish.

"It has not done all that was asked of it, but it has not done badly, even in the quantity of the houses it has erected - the number up to the end of 1929 was 4,913 - and the quality of dwelling it has provided and done excellently. It may be said, indeed, that thanks to the high ideals upon which its Housing Committee has worked, more progress has been made in the ten years it has been setting the fashion in cottage building, than in a couple of generations of pre-war domestic building".

The average rent of houses at this time varied according to type between seven and ten shillings a week though the majority of them were eight and sixpence to ten shillings a week. These figures were of course exclusive of rates.

At the end of 1926 the number of applicants still on the waiting list was about 6,000 with the average number of additions per week increasing by 40 to 50. So, although Braunstone was going to be the largest estate of all, so far, it was fairly obvious that a housing shortage begun in 1919 was still going to continue.

Private Housing Subsidies

BEFORE going on and telling more Braunstone stories, it might be propitious here to mention private subsidy housing.

Without going into the political machinations, the act of 1923 also provided for the grant of lump sums towards the cost of building private houses.

Leicester City Council immediately made itself the medium through which people of the city could obtain such benefits. Grants of up to £75 were made according to the floor areas of houses with the total cost being limited to £675. Under the Scheme, every precaution was taken to ensure that the benefits passed into the hands of the persons for whom they were designed.

Another form of assistance given to the prospective owner of a house to lighten the burden of purchasing was known as the Building Society Guarantee.

The basis of the Scheme was that Building Societies could grant a mortgage on a house up to 90% instead of the usual 66⅔% in those days, the City Council standing as guarantor for the difference between the percentages. This whole Scheme was very advantageous in allowing those people who had the desire to purchase their own house to relieve, to a small extent, the pressure on the Corporation to provide Council housing for the majority.

But now let us go back to Braunstone Estate in the thirties.

Braunstone Post Office and Shop in 1933. Weekly family wage £1.10s.0d to keep a family of four. You could buy 20 cracked eggs for 6d (2¹/₂p), a bag of flour for 6d, Kitchen Scraps for 1d. And pocket money for children? – 1d per week!

41

From unlit streets and
'Ladies of the Night' to the origins of a Tenants' Association

WHEN Leslie Sumner moved into a new house in Rancliffe Crescent in 1932 the estate was, in his words, "in a terrible way". He continued: "This was a new estate with no roads made up, no lights, no causeways, no nothing. In fact, it was because of this lack of basic amenities that we formed what was to be the first Tenants' Association.

"A Mr. Hall, Mr. Bell and Mr. Sherwin, together with myself, called a meeting of tenants and, as a result, we formed the Braunstone Tenants' Association. We used to make a collection monthly of a shilling, which in those days was a lot of money, and from then on we progressed. We brought to the notice of the Corporation what our requirements were and what was wanted but which, of course, they knew about anyway!

still unlit. Well of course, being dark, and human nature being what it is, this little area soon gained itself a name for prostitution. But the lighting that the tenants finally got installed soon squashed all that sort of thing!

"After the association had been formed, we soon got a social side going which all helped to create a communal spirit. I ran the social side myself and one of the first things we formed was a cycling section.

"Everyone threw themselves into the events with gusto. We had concerts, get-togethers, pantomimes, Miss Hope's concert party, Miss Green's concert party, and I think their was another one too, but I can't just bring that to mind.

"These were all held at the Hamelin Road Infant School to begin with, but that wasn't large enough as we grew, so we went to

Unmade roads on the new Braunstone Estate in 1932

"One of the first things we brought to their notice was that after lighting had been supplied to the estate, there was a cul-de-sac leading down to the allotments which was

Folville Rise School where I ran a concert party, a get-together and a whist drive on a regular basis. Every Christmas we used to run what we called a Fur & Feather Whist

Drive. I was in charge of these and they always classed me as the little man with the big voice and, of course, I could shout in those days, covering as many as 100 tables at a time". I then asked Mr. Sumner how his move on to the estate affected day to day planning, shopping and so on.

He said: "Well, when we first came up here I knew this end of the town but there were no shops in the immediate vicinity. Traders use to come round with a horse and cart or a motor and cart and things like that and my wife used to do most of the shopping. There was a Co-op in Mostyn Street but that was a fair distance. When the traders brought our groceries and so on, they would bring the order one week and take the order for the next week, so you paid for the one you got. Then the first shop was opened at the bottom in Redmarle Road. That was Cockins and was shortly followed by G.B. Smith. Of course there was a fish & chip shop but this didn't last long - in fact, it soon went bust. Their name was Smith too". I then asked Mr. Sumner about community relations.

"Well, when I first came here 57 years ago", he mused, "We were all young people with kiddies. Of course, at that time you had to have a kiddy before you got a house; and everyone on the estate was young. Unfortunately, I am now the last one left of the old 'uns, but we were very sociable. Everybody spoke to everybody. Of course you didn't live in each other's houses, but everyone was entirely different socially to what they are today, believe me. In those

days, we used to go visiting to 5 or 6 houses or more, but now, everyone's passed on. So now, I am a bit of a lone soul. I've got a couple of good kids near who moved in

after my wife died 9 years ago, and they're very good to me. So I suppose that perhaps some of the old community spirit could still be developing."

Sitting in his favourite chair in his spotless, comfortably furnished and cosy room, ("I have a Home Help every week"), Mr. Sumner talked about life before he came onto a Council estate.

"Well I suppose I have always had a very comfortable life. I was brought up in a family of three with 9 years between between me and my brother, and so many years between me and my sister. We were brought up in 32 Newport Street. I was born at number 34, but we moved to 32 and from

Mr Leslie Sumner outside his greenhouse

43

then on I went to work as an apprentice cabinet maker for 7 years. When I had finished my apprenticeship, I was like a good many more people who, having had to pay for their apprenticeship, went flat out to make up for it. I started courting, and had the pleasure of marrying the girl. We were married for 57 years.

"I was sort of apart from my brother and sister because they were very well educated. They didn't have a secondary school education, of course, but they were very good scholars and that saw them on their way. Me, I was the other way, I was more for sport. You name it, I tried it. I had very good parents, but I didn't see much of my Dad because he was connected with horses, and you know what it is with horses first thing in the morning and last thing at night. So I can't say we had a lot to do with him. But we were comfortable. I think my father's

wages were 18/- a week, but with a wife and three children to keep he was rather pushed. So my mother went to work as well. I suppose I was what today you would call a latch door kiddy. I used to come home to an empty house, and had my duties to do such as lighting the copper fire and so forth.

"After I was married it was 4½ years before we had a child and then we came to live on the estate. But that was a long, long time ago and now I am not able to get out unless I am taken out. I am very short of breath and I can't walk anywhere. I go to the over-sixties on a Tuesday afternoon and that's about as far as I can walk. To give you a rough idea, I had to go for a hair cut the other week and I said to the Barber, 'Take plenty off, because I can't come here very often!'".

Mr. Sumner is visited regularly by his son and still thinks the estate is great.

Folville Rise School

Fumigation and Bonfires

MR. Pilgrim, of Cuffling Drive, New Parks, not only lived on Braunstone Estate in the early days, he was also an electrician working within the square of Bendbow Rise, Cort Crescent, Hockley Farm Road and Hand Avenue. This was in 1936 and his second job was as an apprentice electrician for George Green. Talking about people in that particular section of the estate, he said that most of them were ex-service people from the First World War who had wanted good homes to start families. "But in North Braunstone, where I also worked, they were rehousing people from the area around what is now St. Margaret's Bus Station".

One of his jobs was to go round to the new houses and the new tenants with a box of lamps for their electric lighting, for which he always had to get a signature. This meant that he was very often in the individual house for quite some time, and he couldn't understand how the tenants could stand the smell of bitter almonds which he presumed was from the prussic acid gas used to fumigate the furniture and bedding. Before prospective tenants could move in to a new Council house, it was customary for their existing furniture to be taken away by the Corporation and fumigated. Not everyone's furniture needed this of course, but it was a general precaution by the Council against the carrying of infection from a previous environment. Mr. Pilgrim continued: "The smell was pretty pungent but at least people knew everything was clean. Of course some people had very nice homes and they made a totally fresh start, but I'm afraid that wasn't so with everybody".

Mr. Pilgrim recalls that when he lived in Braunstone, they had very good neighbours and it was quite natural to pop outside and go and talk to someone and leave the door unlocked, knowing full well that no one would make a quiet entry and depart with the family silver! He particularly remembers weddings, with neighbours helping with crockery; street parties and, particularly, at the end of the war when they had a very big street party with an extremely big bonfire on V.E. day. It was so big that it actually burnt a hole in the tarmac of Newfields Avenue!

> *"...it was quite natural to go and talk to someone and leave the door unlocked..."*
>
> *Mr Pilgrim*

Interlude – 1932

Not the Elton Street slaughterhouse, but a similar situation on City Wall Street – looking down the narrow residential street to Sanvey Gate you can see the gable wall of the slaughterhouse in the middle of the picture.

Elsie, together with her husband and son Fred, moved from Old Milton Street to take over the tenancy of a pub in Dover Street. Here, in the centre of a conglomeration of two bedroomed villas at one end and communal court cottages at the other, was a mix of most of the people who were destined to populate North Braunstone. And it was in this mix, that Fred made his friends - acutely aware, even at the tender age of seven, of the 'us and them' syndrome between villas and court. This naturally affected the children and the odd fight over status was commonplace.

Today, remembering those early years, he has no regrets about being brought up in the area. He learned quite a lot about human nature at an early age and looks back with something akin to affection when he compares the attitudes of those embryo

Council house people with the commercial minded attitudes of today. In those days, in spite of the living conditions and the almost breadline existence, the families exuded a contradictory mix of camaraderie and pride; love and hate; yet, in times of trouble, a neighbourly closeness and caring; the closing of ranks is a common cause.

Fred was sent to St John the Divine Junior School, where he soon fell foul of Mr Wheatcroft, the Head, and quickly learned the value of his different canes. They ranged from thick to thin and were used according to 'the crime'. They were all pretty hard, but the thin red one was the one that struck most terror into the heart and taught discipline quickly; and it was no good holding your hand at an angle for the cane to slide off - a rap underneath the

hand soon brought it horizontal again!

Slaughtering day was a red letter day in the school week. The slaughterhouse in Elton Street was almost next door to the school and was part of a terraced row of cottages, either side and facing. By today's standard of hygiene, the slaughterhouse and cottages would be branded as untenable. On the days of slaughtering, the slaughterhouse doors were opened, letting out the smell of meat and blood. And after the killings, the bloody floor was washed down, with diluted blood spilling into the gutters in the street. Hardly a healthy situation and one which, today, would not be tolerated. But for the boys and girls from St John's their only concern was not to miss the slaughter. The beast was usually pulled up on a rope and they watched with almost

'Vicky Park' showing the Pavilion and War Memorial. The trees on the right were our cricket stumps. The Pavilion was eventually destroyed by a bomb in the 1940s.

hypnotic fascination as the slaughterer with his large pole axe stunned the beast with a resounding blow. After the slaughter, the lads went off to perform a metaphoric slaughter of their own.

In those days, religion played an important part in their lives. Poor they may be; rough they may be; but God was a name to be spoken of with reverence; and His Commandments (or almost all of them) were obeyed to the letter. To the letter that was, until someone mentioned 'Holy Cross'; this was the rallying cry for the Church of England to battle with the Church of Rome. And battle they did, too, chasing down New Walk to meet the enemy. But it all ended amicably. No-one got hurt. No-one really bore malice. It was just another way of getting something out of the system. And on a Saturday, Roman Catholic played happily with his Church of England 'foe'!

Still on a religious theme,

Whit Sunday invariably dawned hot and dry. The streets were dusty, while the flotsam from the night before swirled around in the eddies created by the occasional zephyr.

Around mid-morning, folk began to gather in groups outside their cottages, the doors wide open to try and let in a little air; while the halfboard was across the door to keep the toddlers and babies in. Then came the sound of music, and the procession from Holy Cross, with the young girls all dressed in white, would come round the corner of Chatham Street and process up Albion Hill. It was soon all over, however, and at 12 O'Clock the men drifted to

A rare day out – Elsie and sister Bertha living it up

the 'Dani', Black Boy or Dover Castle.

During the school holidays 'Vicky' Park was a Godsend. Although it was only 15 minutes up New Walk, groups went off to spend the day as though they were going on safari. With bottles of liquorish water made by the simple expedient of shaking up liquorish sticks in the bottle, and with what food or sweets could be spared, off they would go. Home-made cricket bats and their sister's ball would provide the fun, and when they tired of this, they simply laid down and enjoyed the sun.

Fag Cards. Tin Can Lurky. Weak 'Osses and Tram 'Osses - these were the games that lads (and sometimes girls) were made of. And in the evening, just to provide a diversion, they would tie the doorknobs of the villas together with string; knock on both doors and wait for the occupants to try and open them. Sometimes the string broke. Then, it was everyone for themselves!

On Saturday mornings, for the lucky ones, it was a visit to the Picture House and the 'Tuppenny rush'. And if their luck continued to hold, perhaps a trip to see 'City' play in the afternoon.

Saturday night was a night of fish and chips and fights.

For the kids it was a penny worth of chips and a few 'Bits', while for the men and occasionally the women it was a trip to one of the pubs. Around 9 o'clock, Fred found himself pushed off to bed, expected to sleep through the noise and revelry coming through the floor from the rooms below. But when the pub closed at 10pm, he was to be found kneeling on a chair looking out of the window and waiting for the fun. This was inevitably a fight between the two same protagonists, the weekly row being invariably over the same woman. A crowd would make a ring then, the two men, with coats peeled off, carefully folded and laid on the floor and sleeves rolled up would set to with a vengeance. It was usually over pretty quickly, with perhaps a bloody nose or a bruised lip the only signs of damage. Then, honour satisfied, both men would carefully put on their jackets and, supporting each other, stagger drunkenly up the street!

By 1935/6, most of Fred's friends and their families had moved to North Braunstone, taking with them that community spirit built up in times of adversity and to be nurtured in their new surroundings. The wreckers moved in on Dover Street and, even though trade was slumping, Fred's parents continued to keep the pub going. Eventually, though, they had to sell the tenancy back to the brewery, and with only a few pence to their name after all debts had been paid, moved into rented accommodation in the West End. Fred's parents then went to work for publicans with whom a few short months previously they had been on equal terms and Fred was left to his own devices. Each night he would come home from school and get his own tea and then go out on his paper round. This was the second round of his day, the first one having been early morning. On a Saturday he would work in the grocer's packing up people's orders and delivering them on the grocer's bike. After his final paper round on Saturday night he would get his money which, together with his grocery money and a few free groceries, he would give to his mother to go towards the housekeeping.

Fred now knew better than ever how many of his friends had lived; for his lifestyle was much the same as theirs had been - the whole family scrambling for every penny; pork scratchings and polony for Saturday dinner; waiting for the market to close on a Christmas Eve to try to get a cheap bird for the 'morrow - even fish and chips was a treat. But with pigs' and sheeps' heads, a few vegetables and some culinary know-how, a family didn't need to starve.

War came and his parents moved back to their beloved Belgrave. Fred joined the Navy soon after his seventeenth birthday and lost touch with his friends; he never saw any of them again.

The Great Divide
and Pride and Prejudice

IN carrying out its scheme of slum clearance in the Thirties, the Housing Committee unwittingly created a class situation that was to be blown out of all proportion in the years to come; a situation that paralleled the 'Irish Reputation' referred to at the beginning of this sketch in 'Interlude 1858'.

When the original Braunstone Estate, later to become Braunstone South, was built, the fairly high rents charged by the Corporation, meant that only the artisan and skilled worker with reasonably high wages could afford to move in. Given the healthy environment of a new estate with tenants of a like mind, as it were; with houses - luxurious by Inner City standards - and a green belt to boot, and a park - theirs to hold in perpetuity, it was not surprising that in a few short years, Braunstone became a 'superior' estate.

But whilst this cosy situation was developing, the Housing Committee, looking at ways and means of housing the poorer families to be evacuated from the City slums, decided to build a cheaper form of house which was well within the pockets of the unskilled worker and labourer.

They chose an area north of Braunstone Park and proceeded to build. Thus, the 'Great Divide' was created: North of the Park, the poorer families; and to the South, the richer ones.

It is said that give a dog a bad name, and sooner or later it will live up to expectations. In the case of Braunstone North, the bad name was there from Day 1. Good or bad, all the tenants were labelled 'Trouble makers' and this was reflected not only in the attitude of adults, but also in their children.

However, to set the scene, let us first look at the childhood memories - most certainly coloured by adult tales - of Mrs. Stadler, in

> *"They chose an area north of the Park and proceeded to build. Thus, the great divide was created..."*

Fishing at the sluice-gate. Braunstone Park – long before the estate was built.

49

those days, a 6-year old child living on Ratby Lane, but now happily living on a City Council Estate.

She said: "It was in 1935 that I remember the North Braunstone Estate being built. All the countryside had been cleared to make way for the houses and only two spinneys were left, and these soon began to disappear as trees were chopped down for firewood. I think the people came from the Wharf Street area.

"On a Sunday morning, I used to stand at our gate watching different men go to the Airmen's Rest Pub, which had only just been built. They were dressed in black caps, white scarves and always accompanied by a greyhound. And you could always hear them coming back! It was certainly a different way of life to ours on the Lane.

"Being only 6 at the time, I can't remember too much about the houses, or what went on. But I do know that as

children we were warned not to go near Gallards Hill; it was supposed to be notorious; but it was the black caps and mufflers - almost like a Regiment - that even today sticks in my mind.

"I know there used to be some very weird stories going about in those days and the Estate had a really bad name. Of course, I was only a small girl, and that generation has now passed on and the Estate has improved tremendously".

The following interviews were with tenants who moved into North Braunstone in the Thirties. On the generally held view of notorious and weird, you must make up your own mind:-

Mrs. Allen of Baron's Way, Netherhall, moved to Raven Road, Braunstone, as a child from Navigation Street. Speaking of life in Navigation Street, she said:

TOP:
In the back garden at Raven Road with mum

BOTTOM:
Mrs Stadler

"From what I remember, there were about eight to ten houses in one yard, one toilet at the end of the yard, and come Saturdays, especially in the Summer, there would be one big tin bath which was filled with water and everyone used to bathe in it. The first one to go in was, of course, very clean, but if you were last, then you were certainly bathing in dirty water. On light nights after your bath, you would put on a nightdress, or more likely dad's old shirt, and you would sit on the front step talking to other children while parents sat outside in chairs.

"On the corner just across Archdeacon Lane was Kemp's shop and I remember we used to go up 3 steps to get in. It had a little half door and Mr. Kemp used to sell little

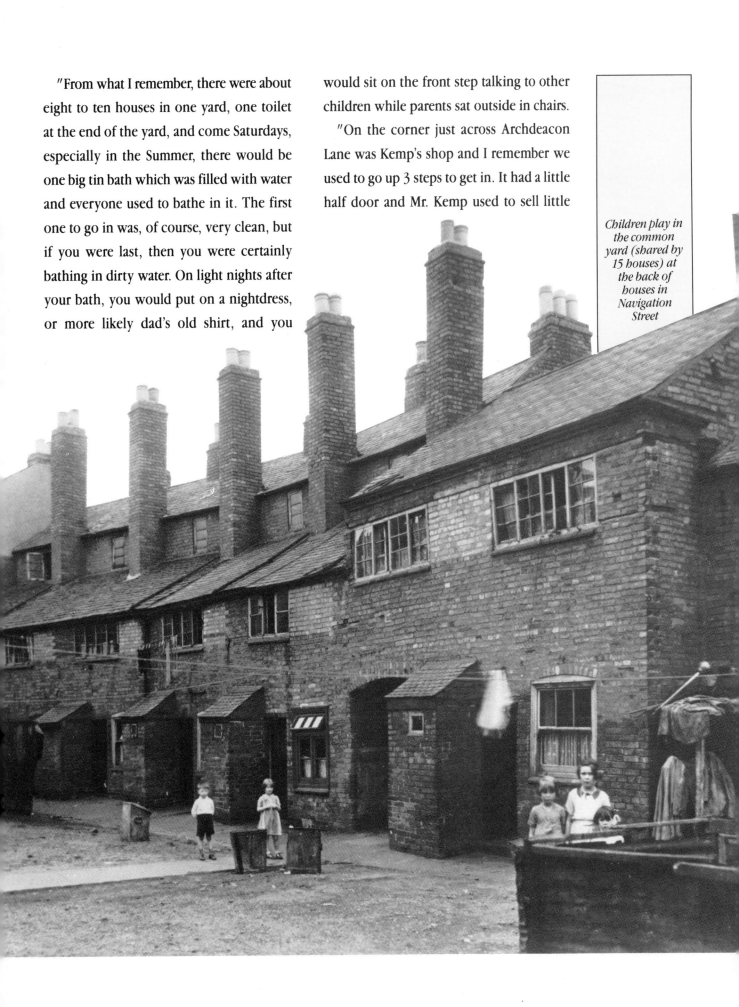

Children play in the common yard (shared by 15 houses) at the back of houses in Navigation Street

iced lollies for a halfpenny. We fared quite well compared to other kids because we had good parents, even though there were a lot of us. My dad worked at the Gas Works at the bottom of the street and he would always give us a penny on a Friday night. But if, of course, you asked for it, then you didn't get it! It was 'if you ask you don't get, and if you don't ask you don't want'. But you always got it, and a little penny cake as well.

"We had to take it in turns to take his breakfast down to the Gas Works, and you would go up these rickety old iron stairs going round a hot pipe running up the centre.

"In Archdeacon Lane, just along the road was Wheelers the Removers, which had an iron bar outside where the horses were tethered and drays were unloaded. At the corner of the next street was the 'Keys' pub.

"Then there was Black Hetty. She used to live in a big yard in Charter Street. She always wore a big hat and was always wearing black. She never spoke to anyone and it was all very weird. Everyone called her Black Hetty and everyone was a bit scared of her. I don't think she would do anyone any harm, of course, but she was one of those peculiar people, and we kids kept right away!

"Our area was a great community. Everyone helped each other.

"Up to the age of 9 life was great. But then they started pulling the houses down and the old buildings and we were never allowed to go out of the street, except when we went to school in Caroline Street.

"There was one big hall in the school with a room at the bottom where they took in children of 2. My sister went to school

With dad in the garden: "But once the back garden was organised you daren't set foot in it. Dad grew his own food there and woe betide anyone who interfered."

"I was 9 when we moved to Braunstone and I shall never forget it. There were 3 of us pushing an old pram loaded with boxes and things, pots and so on. We walked all the way to Braunstone, at least 5 miles.

"Until now, we had never been out of the district beyond Belgrave Gate, so before we went, Dad wrote down instructions on how to get to Braunstone.

"Walking up the Shoulder of Mutton Hill with a pram was very hard work, but being youngest I came off lightest. I remember near Braunstone Park there used to be a big iron gate in front of a house where old man Walker lived. It was there that I picked up my first acorn".

Speaking of her changed environment, Mrs. Allen went on:

"Oh! it was good. You had freedom.

"The first night we moved into the house we had nothing to sleep on (presumably being fumigated). There were no shops, no fences round the back-gardens, no roads, no buses - not anything. Even those who went to work in the morning had to walk down to the tram at Western Park, and I remember on the first night my brother Jack got lost.

"We were all worried stiff and then I remember somewhere in the back-garden Jack was shouting: 'Mam'! and our Mam said: 'Oh you b.....', that's our Jack'. And then we all went mad. It was really great. But once the back-garden was organised, you daren't set foot in it.

"My dad grew all his own food there and woe betide anyone who interfered.

at the age of 2 and with the exception of dinner-time, we used to be there all day. But in the afternoon we used to have to go to sleep on metal beds. Every morning we used to go to the cloak-room and we had to wait at the door facing the headmistress's desk. She was a right so-and-so. You had to have your handkerchief neatly pinned to your pinafore and if it wasn't, oh dear! The school was really split into 3: there were the babies at the bottom end, then the infants and finally the juniors. They were all different classes but there was certainly no noise. You simply just learned your lessons.

With my sister Peggy and our dog

53

Bendbow Rise over 50 years ago – oak trees and open space

"Bendbow Rise was smashing. There were all oak trees down there, where the Oak stands now. Nobody broke them, they were lovely old trees. And all around was beautiful green grass. What made the Council eventually cut them down I do not know. The Green is still there; the only difference is that they have now built a Neighbourhood Centre on it.

"Every Saturday, I would go into Braunstone itself. It was a great place, but when people knew that we had come from North Braunstone we were immediately put down. To say you lived on Braunstone meant that you were nothing.

"There were no schools as such, only a little wooden place on Bendbow Rise. But it was so over-crowded, that we eventually had to go to Hinckley Road School until they built the one at Cort Crescent, which was 4 wooden classrooms with no fence around the playground.

"Whilst we were waiting for the 4 classrooms to be built, we continued to go to Hinckley Road. I hated that school. All the people from 'the other side of the fence' were all dressed nice. But they were no better than us really and at least, we were clean. Also, you never got the language from us that you got from the 'others'. With the South Braunstone people it was a case of 'us' and 'them'.

"Another example was my sister Blanche. She won a scholarship, but because of our situation, Mum couldn't even afford a tunic and the teacher really showed her up in front of the others. She never forgot it. She hadn't got a chance, even though she was brainy, because she came from North Braunstone. By the time I got there, things had slowed up a bit, but it still brought the worst out of you."

I asked Mrs. Allen why she thought this should be. She continued:

"I think it was all the fault of the media. They talked of the Council pulling down slums and whilst they were not very good houses, at least they were homes, and they were good homes! It was a case of give a dog a bad name. We never had a lot, but we had good parents and they certainly looked after us."

Mrs. Allen said that she blamed the Council for how they had let things get today. She continued:

"In our day there used to be wooden fences all round everything, and they were never broken down. The streets were clean and all houses were cared for. We were certainly worse off than the tenants today, but they, of course, think they are worse off than we were. But they are not. They just don't seem to know how to stand on their own two feet. But that is the present generation.

"When we first moved into Raven Road, there was no toilet upstairs and chambers used to freeze in the Winter! But they were good houses and they are good houses now. It is awful to see them being run-down. And there doesn't seem to be any community spirit like there was in those days.

"When we moved into the Estate we had all come from the same area and we brought our community spirit with us. It was a nice community. There was a nice family atmosphere. It was a new environment and we certainly made the most of it and developed it. Yes, they were great people, but I am afraid to-day the situation has changed terribly. It really started after the War.

"When we were married we moved into Willow Street - that was our first home. It was where the old houses stood facing St. Matthew's Estate. I suppose we were lucky to get it with my son being only 15 months' old, but really I hated the place. We lived in No. 67 and outside at the back we had French windows with a little verandah. Then there was a wall; and behind the wall were the dustbins. Why the Council built them like that goodness only knows. The youngsters would never go round the wall to put the rubbish in the bins, over the wall it would go! My husband used to go round every Saturday morning and tidy everything up. I knew then, what it meant when people said houses developed into slums. Houses become what people make them. Of course, I don't think that the Council is hard enough on tenants, not like they were with us when we lived at Braunstone. There, if you did anything really bad you were out on your neck. Today's people think they have got a lot, but really they have got nothing because they will never know the companionship of the old Estates as we knew them."

TOP: *Children's VE Day party on Raven Road.*

BOTTOM: *"Every Saturday I would go to Braunstone itself." A typical footpath across the park, from the estate to the village, 30 years ago.*

55

Sunday School
and the Plymouth Brethren

"...We had an allotment at the end of our garden, and during the war, rabbits, chickens and even bees were kept there."

MRS. Smith, now living in Leicester Forest East, came to Leicester from Malvern with her parents and, in 1929, and moved into a house on Winstanley Drive.

Mrs. Smith continued:

"We were very excited to get this Council house. We moved in during the Winter. There were no roads, no lights and the house was very very damp. But the wonderful thing about it was that we had a bathroom and toilet upstairs, which was very unusual in those days. But to have a bath with hot water and a gas boiler in the kitchen, it was marvellous! But it was often very cold, our only heating being just two fires. We had a parlour house which had 2 rooms and a kitchen downstairs, with a fireplace in each room. But only one of the rooms was used. The other was kept for

special occasions. The room we lived in had a fire which didn't particularly throw out much heat, but we were much tougher in those days than folks are now!"

I then asked Mrs. Smith what the people were like.

"Well," she mused, "We were all about the same, very basic working-class people. My father worked for the Midland Red Buses as a driver. My mother did not go to work. I went to school on Hinckley Road, Dovelands, and I had to walk there either through the allotments at the back of our house, or up Winstanley Drive, down Shoulder of Mutton Hill and catch a tram at the terminus to school. At this time neither road nor pavements were made up. In Winter, it was pretty grim. The nearest way of getting into town was to walk down to Western Park and catch a tram. The nearest doctor who we used was at Western Park. My mother was rather delicate and poorly and, to get her medicine, I had to catch a

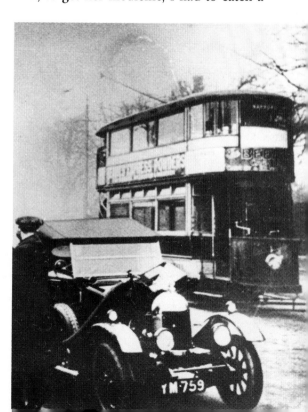

TOP: Mrs Smith – happy memories of Braunstone Park and the Sunday School

BOTTOM: " The nearest way to get to school was to walk down to Westen Park and get a tram."

56

tram from the bottom of Hinckley Road to the Dispensary. It wasn't very pleasant at all.

"As far as I can remember, I think the roads were finally completed in 1931-32. After that, we had some very old-fashioned one-man buses on the Estate.

"When I left Hinckley Road School I went to Alderman Newton's Girls' in town, just about the time we had these buses, and it was easier, much easier to get to school in town.

"We had very good neighbours both sides of us. One was a very big family of about 6, and we were all friends together, because it was such a bleak place. There were no shops until you got down to Hinckley Road and Mostyn Street, not like the other Braunstone Estate. They built the road first and then the houses. I remember Braunstone Park. When I wasn't at school, my mother and I used to take the dog a walk and watch the rabbits.

"We had an allotment at the end of our garden, and during the War, rabbits, chickens and even bees were kept there. It was lovely in the Summer."

In her recollections of the past, one of Mrs. Smith's happiest memories was of Sunday School: "When I first went to live on Winstanley Drive, there were no Sunday Schools at all. But then Mr. Bond, who lived on Rancliffe Crescent, decided to start one in his front room. As the class grew the room got very crowded, and we moved to Folville Rise School.

"Mr. Bond was a member of the Plymouth Brethren, and from the small beginnings of his front room, Braunstone Avenue Hall developed. I had some lovely times there, and eventually Mr. Bond was joined by a Mr. Thomas from Gooding Avenue."

Smiling at the memory, Mrs. Smith continued:

"I used to play the organ for the babies' class when I was about 12, and, together with Mr. Bond's daughter, we used to take a class of 'very small ones'. I well remember pedalling the organ like mad!"

Winstanley Drive from Hinckley Road junction

57

"The only way I shall leave
is when they carry me out"

"But in spite of all my moans and groans, I wouldn't leave this house if we were offered anywhere else in Leicester to live, rent free..."

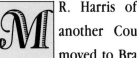

R. Harris of Gallards Hill is another Council tenant who moved to Braunstone in 1938.

"When I was born in All Saints Road, it was quite a good area in those days, especially at night and during the Summer. On a warm evening everyone would sit on the doorsteps talking and there was a great communal spirit. It was the same with my wife, who lived in Newfoundpool. She did the same thing.

"When we got married, we went to live in Johnson Street, off Craven Street. But soon afterwards, the Council decided to demolish the Road. They said that we had to move to Braunstone and there could be a wait of 7 to 8 months. However, there was the corner house on Gallards Hill vacant if we wanted it. So I said, give me the paper, and I will sign. And so it was we came to live on Gallards Hill.

Mr and Mrs Harris

58

"When my wife came up the road, the first thing she said was: 'Oh! look at the size of the windows!'. She then came into the room and said: 'Isn't this big!' And to us everything was big. Big room. Big garden -

it was heaven not to be cramped. It was a bit of a pull to come here though, because we had got our grass roots in the Inner City. However, once we had settled, we really enjoyed it. My wife had the house and I worked really hard on the garden for two years. We really developed the place. When I first came here, I didn't know a dandelion from a carrot. But I soon learned. Today, everyone comes to me for plants but, most of all, I like to give them to the old people.

"When we moved up here we brought two girls with us and after that had four more children. We now have 17 grandchildren and 8 great-grandchildren. And today - as in the early days - we all stick together, but it is like that on the whole Estate. If you had been here on Sunday you would have met all the family.

"In 1938, Gallards Hill was very under-developed. The pavements and roads were not made up. There was no transport - only a tram up to Western Park, and my wife really struggled to push the kiddies' pram over the gravel.

"Across the road were green fields, and up to a few years back we could see Old John from the back bedroom window but, of course, that is all built-up now.

"When the war broke out it seemed as if everybody on the Estate wanted to know everybody and work together. There was certainly a great community spirit. We wanted to fight together and win together. And that spirit, nurtured during the War, remained afterwards - at least with us older ones.

"Mainly through the efforts of our generation, the Estate got its Recreation Centre, Neighbourhood Centre, Resource Centre and a Jubilee Centre for the kiddies. But it hurts me when I see the lack of interest shown by the younger generation. They don't seem to bother as we did. But, perhaps, things come too easy these days. In 1974 for example we started a carnival and made a lot of money. Thousands of people used to attend. It ran for ten years. But not anymore. The young one's haven't bothered to carry it on. But we can still stand together when we want. You take this road with its dual-carriageway. It is splitting the Estate in two. We tried for years, as a Community, to stop this happening. We were unsuccessful, but at least we tried".

Still on the subject of Community spirit:

"In 1951 the Estate decided they wanted a Club. We simply pooled all the work resources on the Estate and the men built it

themselves in Cantrell Road in their spare time - just like that! But that was 40 years ago. Would it happen today?" Tom mused.

After a pause, he smilingly continued:

"But in spite of all my moans and groans, I wouldn't leave this house if we were offered anywhere else to live in Leicester rent free. Its a nice corner, and a nice section of the Estate".

At this point Mrs. Harris took over.

"My husband has told you what it was like when we moved from Johnson Street where we were sharing a wash-house and toilet. To come up here and find you had a gas copper and a bath was Heaven to us, and in no way would I like to leave. If someone said to me

we are going to put you into your own house and you can live there rent-free, as my husband said: 'No way!'. I would never leave North Braunstone. We have lived here for 42 years, and I cannot fail it. Out of this road we are the only original ones left. We all came to the Estate together, but in the meantime many have just died. Now we have very different people. Mind, there's a lovely family next door, with two sets of twins. They would love to buy their house. I wish in years gone by that we could have afforded to buy ours, but no way could we have done that with six children."

Mrs. Harris is an extremely genuine person, and she certainly showed it by her final comment:

"If it is any consolation to anyone outside who likes to call North Braunstone, then they had better come and live here to find out. Because if it is any recommendation, the only time I shall go is when they carry me out!"

TOP: Braunstone Park in Jaunary 1953 – "cleaning up" ready for the spring show of daffodils and crocuses.

BOTTOM: The village blacksmith in about 1870. "I used to walk with my elder sister over to Braunstone Village and the Blacksmith's shop

60

The final word

IN conclusion, let Mrs. Janet Setchfield, Ward Councillor for North Braunstone, and a former Lord Mayor of the City and someone who was brought up and still lives in Braunstone have the final word on 'The Great Divide' and 'Pride and Prejudice':

"My first memory of Braunstone is the park, the fields and the concrete roads beyond. This was in the early 30's when, on a Sunday morning, I used to walk with my elder sister over to Braunstone village and the blacksmith's shop, picking mushrooms en route. Little did I know then, that many years later I would be walking those roads and becoming closely involved with the Community that was to grow up there.

"I have had the privilege and honour of representing North Braunstone on the Council since 1970. I remember my first argument with the then Tory-controlled City Council was over the way they were carrying out the first home improvements - giving families an inside WC, by taking space from the bedrooms which, because the house were built under the 1930 Rehousing Act and therefore had smaller rooms than under any other Housing or Planning Act, meant that the rooms became even smaller! Also they were altering the backdoors to the side of the houses. This meant that you had to walk around the side and through the backgate to get into the back garden. Sinks were put behind the backdoors. There was no work being done to the outside brickwork and no insulation. Everyone was being told that the cause of the mould growing on their walls was condensation. But we won - insulation and proper ventilation was installed and the mould disappeared!

"I have, over the years, objected to Housing Allocation Policy, as North Braunstone appeared to be treated differently to other Estates and the decision to advertise 'Properties to Let' did not help the situation. But at last we got what we wanted, proper improvements to the properties - and that at least was a start. But now the future is uncertain.

"The various parts of North Braunstone that have been recently improved are superb, but there are many good folk still trying to cope with homes built over 50 years ago; homes that have had very little improvement carried out - many still with outside WC's.

"The division between North and South Braunstone with one of the most beautiful parks, not only in the City but in the Midlands, instead of uniting Braunstone has somehow divided it. Perhaps Braunstone Park holds the key!"

61

Little Stories on their own

From Mrs Branston - Saffron

I T was on a very cold day in 1926 when we came to live in Saffron Lane - our very first house. Bill and I were 24 years old and our son was 2½ years.

"The house was at 105 The Fairway and there was a blizzard blowing all over our bits and pieces on the lorry the day we moved in. The roads were not made up and we had to help push the lorry out of the ruts, with our shoes being sucked off our feet. But in spite of cold wet feet and sleety snow blowing in our faces, we didn't mind, for this was to be our 'Seventh Heaven' of a home.

"But when we saw this drab, concrete house surrounded in churned up mud, my enthusiasm went quite a lot. But Bill, ever the optimist, had future plans and straight away stuck a piece of wild ivy near the front door - and it took root too! Bill and I set up the bed first before it became dark, because the electricity had not been connected up. Down in the large room our prized, second hand, horse hair furniture: an old-fashioned well polished table and my bright coloured pegged rug, looked as lost as we felt. The cooker had not arrived and we had to light a fire of wood to boil some water to make a cup of tea.

"Coal was rationed to a 1cwt. at a time, it being the general strike. We had to fetch our rationed coal from the railway sidings at Knighton Fields Road at the top of the hill. Also, we could queue up at the gas works for the same amount of coke. We had to use the pram to collect the coal and coke, because it cost 2/6d to hire a barrow.

> *"I remember coming home one day to find the workmen had moved our lawn."*

Another night in the cold?

Anyway barrows were too heavy for women and children to push up the hill.

"Most people were in the same plight and their houses were candlelit at night, hence the estate was known as Candletown or Chinatown.

"There was only a small 'Co-op shop' on The Fairway and they had a monopoly and would charge accordingly. So we had to traipse down to Saffron Lane to the small shops there for most of what we needed.

"There were no Corporation bus services at the time so we had to walk to the top to the Midland Red bus stop, sometimes soaked with rain, only to find the bus was full.

"These houses were very damp and no matter how often the red tiles were scrubbed, they always dried up white. Our beds felt cold and damp until our bodies warmed the bed clothes. I remember seeing frost shining on the bedroom walls. Still this was our first home, and we were very proud of our front garden full of flowers and at the back the vegetables were showing promise.

"I believe it was about a year after that when the shops on the lane improved, then Corporation bus services started on the estate and I decided to start back work on Abbey Park Road.

"I remember coming home one day to find the workmen had moved our lawn. They said we had too much soil and they needed it for someone else. Bill was raving mad! But when we had the cooker and the wonderful electric light, everything seemed brighter all round.

"Then there was the old bus route over the level crossing, very often with a herd of cows or sheep sauntering in front of the bus. Many a 'lock out fine' they cost me! After a while, there was a new bus route cut out of the hillside and the railway bridge was built too. My boys, along with others, would spend hours watching the workmen down below darting about like ants on a dungheap.

"Then came Marriot Road School with its wooden built classrooms for tiny tots and their beloved teacher, Mrs. Gentle and dear old Miss Parker for the older ones. St. Christopher's Church was built and all my five children in turn attended the Sunday School and were christened at the Church.

"Few people had a wireless in those days, I bought one from Wigfalls for 1/6d a week. My boys would bring in their friends to listen and they sang the Ovaltine song with great gusto.

"Children were not so cheeky then, and vandalism was unheard of because most mothers taught their children to respect

You could find room for a few plants in city back yards, but on the new estates there was plenty of room for "front gardens full of flowers" and back gardens full of vegetables

other people's property. In fact, if your child broke someone's window, then the parents would pay for it.

"Now came Linwood Lane School for the older children and Southfields Drive School, also with its wooden huts, for the tinies.

"The new cemetery was a favourite walk for us young mothers with prams, and strangely enough to sit there on the seats, even in that setting, the growing flowers were a treat to behold. Trees were planted on the grass verges, and I wondered would I be alive to see them grow tall. Well they have matured and so have I! Then came the swings and seesaws, also shelter huts where we young mothers could sit and drink cups of tea and watch the little ones at play. But now, the vandals have come and pulled them down. I wonder what satisfaction it gave their little minds to rob the tinies of their enjoyment, and doesn't it give a very good example of growing up?

"Then came the W.M.C., beloved by men mostly and anyway there were shops now. A lovely library, Co-op guild, evergreen clubs for the grandparents who have watched Saffron grow out of a sea of mud.

"When I look down Windley Road on a summer's day and see the avenue of wonderful trees, I thank the Lord that I am still alive."

From Mr. E.M. Lant, Chaucer Avenue, Littlehampton, Sussex.

A FEW Leicester Mercury's have come our way and I notice the request for information about Leicester's housing estates. If I can help I will. I was born in Chartley Road in 1914 and can well remember the layout of the Narborough Road/Imperial Avenue area with the farms and allotments, also the Braunstone Fields where the large estate is now. It was our play area. We went to live in Peveril Road (the park end round 1929 time) and lived in the area as development went on.

"Nature walks from Narborough Road School Juniors went through the Braunstone Fields too.

"I saw the whole area grow and the countryside recede to where it is at the moment in the Lubbesthorpe area, once a peaceful spot.

"We were last in the city last Tuesday (28th November, 1989) and were amused to see signs saying 'Braunstone, turn on the new bypass' and 'Fosse Park at the M1 Junction'. Fosse Park to us is still in Fosse Road North. It had swings and seesaws for children, which 'Winchester Park' did not have!

"Nature walks from Narborough Road... I saw the whole area grow and the countryside recede..."

64

A Council House out of a hat

EIGHTY year old Grace Smith lives on Gypsy Lane in one of seven houses owned by the Council. According to Grace, the houses were originally built for private development. But after the 1921 strike and with money in short supply, the builder went bankrupt and the Corporation bought the properties and completed the building.

Grace came to Leicester with her parents when her father's Company moved to Barkby Lane. "Of course," says Grace, "There were no houses here then and you couldn't afford to buy, not like you can today. So our first home was three empty rooms in a house on the corner of Loughborough Road. We stored our left over furniture in the cellar."

With the argument that by moving their Company to Leicester they had brought prosperity and work to the town, the Company's Director approached the Corporation to see if they could make any Council houses available to those employees who had moved down with them. When the Corporation offered two on Gypsy Lane,

it was decided to put the names of the oldest employees in a hat and draw two out. "And that," says Grace, "is how I came to live in Gypsy Lane". As she continued: "When we moved in, it was lovely. That year was a long hot summer and we thought we were in Heaven. It was all green fields over there where the Estate is now, with cows in the fields, corn and everything. There were no buses. To get into town, you had to walk to Melton Road or Victoria Road East.

"One of the banes of mum's life was cooking. There was no electricity in those days, only gas. But to get a gas cooker took ages. The 'Cooker' in the house, was something to be seen to be believed. It was heated by the fire and had an oven on top. My mum was a good cook but she couldn't cook a thing on it. My dad had never had so many burnt offerings in all his life - and he loved his food! But, eventually, we got a gas stove and life wasn't too bad. But when I compare the cooker with the cookers of today, it was a monstrosity! But we survived.

"In the beginning, the garden was awful. My father was a dedicated gardener who had been used to a workable garden. But here, workable was the last word you could call it. First, the builders had left a big chunk of concrete in the middle of the garden and my brother and I had an awful time cleaning up the mess. Also, the three spitfuls of top-soil had disappeared. Down the road was a nursery, and it wasn't hard to imagine where the top-soil had gone! But dad made it up. He had loads of manure, courtesy of the Corporation!

"After much debate it was agreed that a grate had been installed... and that what had been done for one person should be done for another..."

Mrs Grace Smith – 80 years young

CITY OF LEICESTER
MUNICIPAL
HOUSING

J. S. FYFE A.R.I.B.A
HOUSING ARCHITEC
LEICESTER. NOV. 193

REFERENCE
Railways and Stations
Corporation Tramway Routes
Corporation Omnibus Routes
City Boundary
Divided into half mile squares
Scale

"Going back to the cooker, mum wasn't satisfied. So she kept pestering the Corporation. I know we got a gas cooker eventually, but in the meantime, mum learned something that made her furious. She learned that someone in Humberstone Drive had had a grate installed by the Corporation.

"This information came about in a coincidental way.

"Dad was an ardent socialist, and each week he used to pay his dues and demands to a female collector. In passing, she commented that her husband - who worked for the Corporation, had recently installed a grate in a house in Humberstone Drive. This was all the information my mum needed. She was fed up with her existing grate. To clean it, you had to carry out all the pieces of iron and clean them. It was really hard work. But armed with the information, she went along to the Corporation and insisted on seeing the head man. Apparently, the head man wasn't available, so she said: 'In that case, I'll wait!' Time went on, so she said to the person behind the counter,: 'Look, it's no good

saying you haven't done anything. I know that you have installed a grate in a house in Humberstone Drive, I know the number and I know the name. What are you going to do about it?' After much debate, it was agreed that a grate had been installed in Humberstone Drive, and that what had been done for one person, should be done for another. Eventually, we bought a grate on my mother's 60th birthday, it cost us £10.00 off Humberstone Road, and the Council fixed it and they also fixed the back boiler. Consequently, we eventually had, because of this, a sort of central heating.

"Because of the pipes running around the room, the bedroom upstairs used to be lovely and warm, the heat coming through the floor.

"When we came into these houses initially, they were terrible. On the doors there wasn't a bit of paint. It was stained brown, like creosote.

"About three years ago the Council wanted to modernise the house. But as I am eighty odd, I said that I couldn't stand it and I told them I had no intention of moving out of the front to live in the back. I couldn't

FACING PAGE:
By 1935 suburban council housing was growing all round the city

ABOVE:
Originally a private development, Mrs Smith's house on Gipsy Lane was taken over by the Council in 1921

67

do this at my age, and that was all there was to it. Next door, they have lovely central heating but that doesn't matter. However the Council did do a bit to mine, new doors, piping etc, new chimneys and new fences and they charged me £2.00 a week extra on the rent. Of course I wanted everything that everyone else had had, but quite frankly at my age I couldn't stand the mess and you know what the Council are, it is you have all or nothing!

"Recently, a Council official came down to see if there was anything wanted doing. I told him that my taps were hard to turn off and could I have new ones. He looked and said: 'What you want is some new pipes and taps. Wouldn't you like a nice new sink unit?' Grace continued: 'I said that I had only got an old Butler's sink, and that I would love an new sink unit. So he said that he would get me one. Now, I have got a sink unit and I am very happy.

"When my sister died, the house, which had been our joint responsibility, reverted to me. The Council came along and asked me if i'd like a bungalow. But I pointed out

that I wasn't moving out of this house, because I love gardening - mind you in those days I could do more than I can do now. I said, I am staying here and not moving. So the official said: 'Well, don't worry, we won't move you.' I then thanked her and told her that the only way I would be going out of this house would be in my box.

"Looking back over the years, they have been extremely happy and it certainly used to be lovely until Northfields Estate came upon the scene. Mind you, the people are perfectly alright in the houses that front Gypsy Lane. But it's those in the back ones that have got a bad name. You know, unmarried mothers and all sorts."

Reverting back to her earlier days, Grace recalled groups of parents pushing prams along Gypsy Lane on a Sunday and going to Humberstone for a drink in The Plough. "It was lovely, but there is nothing now. As I have said before there were no houses on Gypsy Lane in those days. In fact, gypsies used to camp there. But I am very happy to have led the life I have and I'm perfectly content to remain where I am".

A back-street shop, similar to the one Barbara knew. Note the communal entry to the court

68

Scratchings, Polony
and a Black Pad

MRS. Barbara Tite lived with her parents in a 'one-up, one-down' in Wood Street in the Wharf Street area of the City. The house was one of seven in a small court with just two communal lavatories.

Mrs Tite wasn't quite four years old when she left Wood Street, but she doesn't ever remember going to either of the lavatories - her mum wouldn't let her, presumably because of the state of them!

She recalls the court vividly. "At one end" she said, "was a sweet factory and at the other end a coal yard".

It doesn't take much imagination to realise what it must have been like in the court on a hot day. One can imagine the sugary smell of the sweet factory and the pungent smell of the coal dust; the whole overlaid by the stifling odour of the court, drifting into the houses through the open doorways.

In the court opposite lived Barbara's friend. They were a big family and Barbara used to think it was very nice to go and play there - particularly when they were in the bedroom dropping matchsticks through the large hole in the ceiling to the room below! When Barbara left Wood Street, she didn't think she would see here friend again. Yet, it wasn't long after settling into their new home that Barbara's old friend came to live at the back of them.

It was just before her fourth birthday when Barbara left the dingy court. One morning, her father came round with his coal cart; loaded up and off they went to their new Council house on Surrey Street, off Catherine Street.

Me with the twins from next door but one and my brother. The factory in the background was A De St Dalmas, who used to make plasters.

"Surrey Street" said Barbara, "was a mix of houses with two and three bedroom council houses and council flats making up the majority". Like most council house people, Barbara remembers pumping water for a bath: "It was really hard work pumping water from the boiler but, instead of having to struggle with coal when we wanted to heat the water ours was gas fired - luxury indeed. But with all the new facilities I didn't mind pumping water for a bath - it was nice to have a bath anyway! All we were concerned about was that we were living in a real house with a garden and everything".

Barbara had fond memories of the boiler, and I asked her why:

"Well, when I was married just at the end of the war, some friends gave us a whole, uncooked ham (with rationing, a luxury). And that was boiled in the copper. Do you know, even today, people talk about that ham".

"It didn't taste of Lux flakes?"

"No, 'cos knowing my mum she would have given it a damn good clean first".

"What about shopping and so on, I imagine in Wood Street you had a corner shop?"

"Yes, we did, but when we moved to Surrey Street we had quite a selection to choose from. In Catherine Street there were Butchers. Bakers. Off-Licences. Grocers and three fish and chip shops".

TOP: *Barbara's Surrey Street home. "All we were concerned about was that we were living in a real house, with a garden and everything."*

BOTTOM: *'Bud' our spotty dog with my brother*

70

"Which was the best fish and chip shop?"

"Well, I can't remember the name but the one on the corner of Bardolph Street was a good one."

"What about other food shops?"

"We had a very good cooked pork shop. Apart from roast pork, they did all sorts of things - jacket and roast potatoes, you name it, everything. Very often we used to get our dinner from there".

"What sort of things, scratchings and polony?"

"Pork scratchings, polony, black pudding, pies - goodness knows what. We may not have had much money, but we certainly lived. I remember there was a clothes shop, drapers and two off-licences - one on each corner. There was just one old fashioned shop on the corner of Surrey Street. It was a good shop, and for everyday things we tended to use that. There were also 'house window shops' - they were really terraced homes with the front room turned into a shop".

Barbara remembers looking across country to the top end of Gypsy Lane. "In those days, Belper Street was the end of the council houses. From there on, it was a big farm and countryside up to Gypsy Lane. They were really good times for us. Playing in the fields, lighting bonfires, walking along the black pad - it was freedom!"

"What was the black pad?"

"Well it was a pad made with black sort of gravel that went past the farm and right on to Gypsy Lane - must have been about three quarters of a mile. But to me, it seemed to go on forever. In fact, I used to think it went to another town!"

"Tell me about your family".

"Well, my sister and brother were both born in Surrey Street. My father was only forty when he died, but we carried on. All three of us were married from Surrey Street. After we left home, mum decided to move to somewhere not so big and got a bungalow in Storn Road. I think she was fairly happy there, but it was such a long way for us to visit her that she looked for somewhere nearer. Eventually the Council gave her a flat on Gleneagles Avenue and when she moved in, she had one of the most pleasant surprises of her life. It may seem strange but her next door neighbour was someone she knew from Wood Street days. So she really settled down then and everyone was happy - happy days!"

TOP: *Mum in the garden*

BOTTOM: *The height of fashion in 1941*

71

New Parks nestles in history

NEW Parks originally formed part of a large section of Leicester Forest, known as the Frith, in which the population of Leicester had certain rights in common. In the Fourteenth Century the area had within it a Foresters' Lodge known as Birds' Nest Lodge. This was rebuilt in 1377 and extensively rebuilt in 1525. By this time it was a noted building with a drawbridge. After New Parks was enclosed in 1526 the moat which surrounded the Lodge survived until the area was built over by the estate about 1950. No doubt this is why a grateful City Council has remembered the occasion in the road on New Parks known as Birds' Nest Avenue!

Today, New Parks is within an area bounded by Groby Road, Hinckley Road and containing, within its environs, Western Park. Up to date, the number of houses built is 3,154, being a combination of bungalows, flats, maisonettes and 2, 3, 4 and 5 bedroomed houses.

Although designated as a Housing area before the Second World War, work on New Parks did not, in reality, start until immediately post-War. The first houses were prefabs. Whether it was an omen for the durability of the houses on New Parks, I don't know, but prefabs certainly had a long life and until they were pulled down by the Council, goodness knows how much longer they could have existed. Perhaps the following story on prefabs gives a clue:

"The first houses were prefabs..."

FACING PAGE:
Aerial view of the developing New Parks Estate in 1950

Typical Council Prefabs, with a life expectancy of 10 years, they were still occupied 24 years later, and still sound

73

Wooden huts
and the Mulberry Harbour

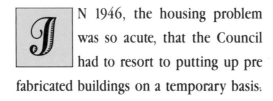

I N 1946, the housing problem was so acute, that the Council had to resort to putting up pre fabricated buildings on a temporary basis.

"Little wooden huts" provided homes for many in the early post-war years

Sectionalised prefabs arriving at Hinckley Road in 1947

Described successively as 'Little wooden huts' and 'Civvy nissans', they were built in 3 main areas: Hinckley Road, Aikman Avenue, New Parks Estate and Ambassador Road, Evington.

A few were also built in Hughenden Drive, Aylestone. All in all, 570 two bedroomed prefabs were erected with an expectancy of 10 years use.

Although not particularly attractive from the outside with their utility construction, they did have one asset: they could be erected quickly and, as far as the Council was concerned, housing people quickly on a temporary basis, was far more important than the appearance of the building. But how wrong can a Council be?

In 1970 - 14 years after their life expectancy, the Housing Committee asked the Housing Manager and the City Architect to prepare a report on the feasibility of keeping the prefabs, particularly in view of their age and the high cost of maintenance. When news of the Housing Committee request leaked out, far from being pleased at the prospect of being rehoused in 'proper houses', the majority of tenants did not want to move!

In a Leicester Mercury article on the situation, the opinion of tenants was made quite clear:

From Letchworth Road, New Parks:

"I have no complaints. I am very happy here. I should hate to leave - mine is a lovely little house. It has all the amenities you could want. Indeed the bungalows are well designed with two bedrooms, a living room, a large kitchen and a separate bathroom and lavatory.

"There is nothing wrong with the place. We have been here for five years and for twelve years before that I was in a flat. I much prefer it here as we are not closed in.

"I know there are other types of houses near us, but there is something different about this place. Most people around here feel as I do about the prefabs and are happy with them".

From Hughenden Drive:

"We moved into our prefab 18 months ago. Previously we had lived in a flat and I had had an illness which made it hard for me to climb steps. I think these places are ideal. They are like private bungalows as they are not joined together, and you can't annoy your neighbours with noise.

"They are warm in the Summer but a little bit cold in the Winter like everywhere else. I think it would be a pity if the prefabs were pulled down".

From Ambassador Road:

"The thought of being rehoused in a bungalow without a garden shocks me. They might as well put me in prison".

He and his wife had moved to Ambassador Road from a three bedroomed house in Coleman Road four years previously and his wife said how happy she was with their present home.

"The prefabs should have a bit of money spent on them for decorating and a few minor repairs. But that is all.

"When our younger son got married we had either got to give up our car or move into cheaper accommodation. So we moved here and we are very happy".

From Hinckley Road:

"We have everything we need here. I would be most upset if I had to move. These prefabs could be made into lovely little homes. All they need is central heating and they would be fine".

Needs Must

In spite of the feelings of tenants, progress could not be halted and the prefabs were finally demolished to make way for 'better housing'. But with their going a part of history went with them.

How the Mulberry Harbour
came to Leicester

*T*HIS story was told to me by Mrs. Payne of Loughborough, who, with her late husband Jim, kept the Fox Hotel for some years after the war.

Mr. Payne, who was a Design Engineer with the Ministry of Defence, was sent to the East India Docks in 1944 to help with the design and construction of what was to become the Mulberry Harbour - the floating dock used off the Northern Coast of France to keep supplies moving for the Allied invasion.

1945 found him involved with the Ministry in the structural design of prefabs. In view of the shortage of building materials, he suggested that the scaffolding used in the erection of the Mulberry Harbour and which was still available, could be utilised in the framework. Thus it was, that by sheer coincidence, the row of prefabs which stood in Hughenden Drive were built with steel tubes that had been associated with one of the most famous inventions of military history.

Mrs. Payne said that her husband was really thrilled with the reaction of the tenants. The prefabs were so lovely and cosy, that when the time came for them to be pulled down, the occupants certainly didn't want to leave them.

Apparently one of the features that Mr. Payne incorporated in the Hughenden Drive houses was some form of air ducting which, as Mrs. Payne says:

"What he designed was, I suppose, an early form of central heating, making everywhere cosy and warm. During the construction of the prefabs he became very friendly with Greville Janner's father who often used to visit him and have a chat about the housing and how it was getting on."

A Coronation bus ride
and night lights for the children

NE of the first people to move into the New Parks Estate was Mrs. Amy Cawdron, of Bonney Road.

Mrs. Cawdron originally lived with her husband and youngest son in two rooms in Argyle Street, off Belgrave Road. She said:

"We were so tight for space that we had the youngest lad in a doll's cot. We went to see Councillor May Goodwin, and within a month we were installed here on Bonney Road. And what a difference it was to Argyle Street, where the house we had was falling down and the only lighting was by gas.

"It was 4 years after the War when we moved into Bonney Road and our only furniture was of the 'utility' kind. But this place was like a palace compared to what we had had.

"Of course we went and had a look at the place before we moved in, and as soon as we saw it, we told the Council without any trouble at all that we would most certainly accept it with gratitude. I know we moved in on a Saturday. There were no pavements, but there was a path to the front door. Our first problem on moving was that we could not find the cot. So we had to borrow one. I was 26 at the time and it was the first time I had ever lived in a house with a bathroom. I know on the day we moved in, I came up by bus and my husband came up with the furniture. I lit a fire and made it up about 4 times, and then turned on the hot tap. I screamed 'God!' there's hot water! I'd never known it before. You see, I had been brought up in the slums of Leicester.

"Having mentioned the words slums of course, one could not call the house we lived in a slum, and I think this is common with lots and lots of people who do move from the Inner Area of the City and have an objection to the houses they left being called slums. But, to get back to New Parks, the problem with the children was getting to school. But when they were older, a bus used to take them to Braunstone School, so I suppose, all in all, it wasn't that bad.

"Although the house was great, one drawback was that there was no side gate. So all us young mothers seemed to spend most of our time looking for lost toddlers in the back garden which, until it was cultivated, was shoulder high with nettles. In those days it was nice, because the 'natural' garden was full of birds.

"Of course, there were no lights up when we first moved in, and I do remember that when the lighting was being installed in the roads, my cousin, who had a house almost facing, said: 'one thing about this lighting, it will be great getting out in the night for the children without having to put the lights on'.

"After we had been in the house for about six months, Council officials came round and checked for faults. And my husband,

> *"...as soon as you mentioned I am a council house tenant, the reaction was "Oh, you keep coal in the bath do you!"*

Bonney Road in the 1950s

being meticulous, had already compiled a list, bless him! He has been dead nearly two years. But he did that archway there, and he did several things to the house to make it like a palace compared to the rooms that we were originally in. We had no central heating and this place was like a barn. The background heating came from wide radiators but they were only about 2 ft. long and weren't really effective. Also, if you valued your hot water, you had to scrape all the tar and such from the fireplaces, and if you didn't keep the pipes clear at the back of the boiler, you didn't have hot water.

"We had quite a nice community spirit in this area. The first people next door to us came from Saffron Lane and we all helped each other out. I remember at the Coronation of Queen Elizabeth, we all clubbed together and collected each week

to lay on a marvellous party for the kids. We hired a Corporation bus to take them a little tour around the City and we bought spoons for them to commemorate the occasion. Funny how these things come back. Of course, you did get the odd rough type of person, but there was no real unpleasantness. Take these trees for example. When they were planted they were only saplings but they have grown, because they were left alone. If you did catch children doing anything wrong, they soon got a clip round the ears.

"Whilst talking of children, there is certainly a change of attitude with the present generation. I blame the Television, and also the parents and people of my generation, because although we were deprived, we didn't realise what we were doing when we went round saying 'I am not going to let my kids go without', and because of this, of course, they have got used to accepting everything given to them as a matter of course. And now, this has gone on to the next generation. Their children, too, are getting more than their parents got. They have no idea of values these days. When I left school at 14 I wanted to work in a flower shop, but no, it was 'All of you go to the factory!'

"Another good example of the community spirit was when coal was rationed. One day, I stood at the Bus Stop

TOP: New Parks Shopping Precinct in 1959

BOTTOM: Mrs Cawdron with the alcove her husband built. "It nearly caused a divorce, but that's another story!"

78

waiting for the special bus, and one of the neighbours said: 'Amy, you look frozen' and I said: 'yes, I've got no coal'. An hour later she was round with a bucketful! They were like that. There are still a lot of us left on Bonney Road, at this end especially, and I think we have all been here 40 years or more. What is it they say, 'better the devil you know than the devil you don't!' Mind you, the City planners want to take a hard look at themselves. You take these bungalows at the back, those down the bottom of the road. They have been built for, and are occupied by, pensioners. But look at the big hill they have to go up to get to the shops and the local Post Office! I worked at the local Post Office for 10 years, so at one time I pretty well knew everyone in the area. Later I worked for the B.S.C., and with being at work all day I tended to lose contact with a lot of people of the Estate. Of course, a lot have died.

"Going back to when we first moved in here, one of the biggest laughs was on the first day. Of course, in Argyle Street we had only had gaslight, so we got ourselves some electric light bulbs, and went up into the bedroom, put one light bulb in, switched on, and nothing happened. Same with the other two bedrooms. The bathroom was the same and yet the downstairs was alright. So we were doing some permutations - you know, switch that one on and we found if the back bedroom was first switched on, the others would work, but all this flummoxed me, especially after gaslight. I suppose it was quite a laugh really. But the Council came around and fixed it. They were very good at fixing things. I have really got no complaints about them. They are quite good now. Usually I find that if you tell them what's wrong, within one to two weeks they

Newly completed houses on the New Parks Estate – the sort of hill the old people have to climb.

are round sorting things out for you. I really love this house. We have had our ups and downs I know, but there is one thing I notice today, and that is that the Council officials are much more polite to us than they were at one time. And this went for other officials too. One got the impression that as soon as you mentioned I am a Council house tenant, the reaction was 'Oh, you keep coal in the bath, do you'. I remember one day, Gavin and I had to go down to the Labour Exchange. We didn't put good clothes on because we had come straight from work. But I certainly didn't like the lady's attitude behind the counter. Eventually I said to her, 'We might be Council house people, but we don't keep coal in the bath.' She said in return: 'Well, I'm afraid that's what we think, Mrs. Cawdron!' Mrs. Cawdron continued: 'Mind you, I think some of the people on Braunstone did that! But going back to the children of today, it doesn't seem that there is any responsibility being bred into them. As I've said before, the trouble

An up to the minute kitchen in the 1940s – Blisset Road on the New Parks Estate

is, they have everything they want and they don't have to struggle for it. I mean, when our children were small, our husbands were on very poor wages, and we used to have to have Kingstone cheques to pay for the kids' clothes, which we repaid weekly with interest. I suppose the principle was pretty well the same as it is with Access today. But when I see my grandchildren, it makes me wonder. They live in Maidenhead and I asked Stephen, my grandson, what he was having for Christmas. He said: 'Don't know grandma, I've got everything'. They both have their own televisions, tape-recorders, computers - the lot. I said, 'well your daddy didn't have all that'. No comment!

"Education was another thing. When our kids passed their 11+, rejoicing knew no bounds. Any kid who had passed his or her 11+ was considered the 'brains of Bonney Road'. Now take my youngest lad. I don't know whether it was a mixed blessing or not, but he passed his 11+ and went to Gateway School. He left there at 18½. He then went to College for 2 years. Studied Economics at the London School of Economics. Met a girl from Petswood. And that was that. He got married, and I see him about 3 times a year. So I don't know whether his passing the 11+ was a good or bad thing!

"I know there was one girl down the road who passed and, oh dear, talk about putting the flags out. According to her family, she *was* the brainiest child in Leicester. I suppose it is natural reaction really, because you see, as kids, we never had the chance to do these

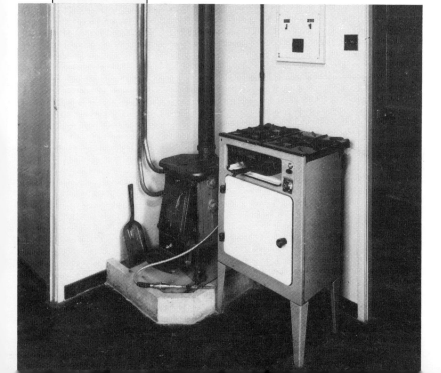

things. My sister, she passed her exams, but Mum wouldn't let her go to Grammar School, so she had to go to Ellis Avenue. By that time she wanted to go into curtain making with Gee Nephews, but they only paid 5/6d a week. And she was told: 'Well you can't go there, after all you can get 10/- a week in a factory'. So I suppose we never got the chance to improve ourselves. Eventually, my sister went into sock making and she was on the dole by the time she was 15. It was really bad in those days, you know. Work was mostly seasonal, but then that was factories".

I then talked to Mrs. Cawdron about what it was like for children growing up and what she thought as a parent:

"Well" she said, "I hope my children had a good balanced childhood. I never had any trouble with them. They had friends and made friends around here. When our Grahame comes home again and he sees any of his old friends, they fall on each others' necks. There was no gang warfare around here in those days, not like today. They just made their own friends and stayed with them."

A damp story

OR obvious reasons, the person who told this story wishes to remain anonymous.

As a girl of 16, she moved into a house on New Parks, having previously lived in a typical inner area house with a communal toilet.

On the first night in the new house, they were without lights - the electricity not yet having been connected up. Their only means of lighting was an oil lamp and when Miss 'X' wanted to go to the toilet upstairs, she asked her sister if she could have the oil lamp. Her sister said: "No you can't, I want it down here. You will have to go up in the dark". So, she said: "I went up the stairs in the dark, found the toilet, and sat down. I started to go and suddenly I was wet through. My legs, my frock, everything. *I didn't know then that toilets had pull-down lids on them!*"

History repeats itself;
Rachmanism adds to the misery; the Council acts yet again

"...in two short years, 1,700 condemned houses had been demolished... rebuilding was going ahead at full speed..."

WITH the building of New Parks Estate, the Council's Housing Department moved into top gear - and not to soon.

Housing waiting lists all over the country had been growing at an alarming rate since 1946 and now, as in 1919, returned veterans were demanding homes for their growing families - mostly conceived through the contingencies of war. The teenagers of 1939 were in their early twenties, and increasing immigration - in many ways comparable to that of the mid 1800's, was adding to demand. But, more importantly, for those in most need of accommodation - the low income groups; the newly weds, the single person looking for work or to improve education; the black immigrant - in fact, anyone without true financial stability, a new word had entered the English Dictionary: 'Rachmanism'! Named after its greatest exponent, Peter Rachman in the London of the 50's and 60's, Rachmanism was the extortion of high rents by unscrupulous landlords playing on the acute shortage of all types of accommodation. Enticing advertisements and a blind necessity for somewhere to live led more and more people into the 'Rachman' trap; to live in single rooms and flats little better,

CITY OF LEICESTER HOUSING DEPARTMENT

FLATS IN AIKMAN AVENUE

or sometimes worse, than the lowest slum. Inevitably, too, the accommodation was not only rundown but, in 9 cases out of 10, totally condemned.

In Leicester, the slum clearances of the 30's - stopped by the war — were quickly resuscitated by the Council and clearance of slum areas recommenced.

Wharf Street was the first area to be cleared and, as the following newspaper reports show, made way for the second biggest estate in Leicester's council house history - St. Matthews.

Such was the impetus give to slum clearance by the Housing, Planning and Estates Committees, that in two short years, 1,700 condemned houses had been demolished and work on rebuilding was going ahead at full speed. By comparison,

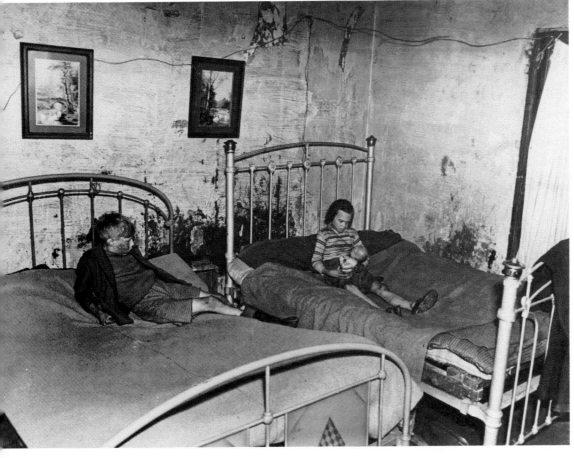

as the newspaper report shows, Nottingham, a City of comparable size, could only demolish 131!

In the following pages a compilation of Newspaper Reports and photographs shows how much was achieved by the Council in housing development between 1952 and 1973. But this should be looked upon as only an introduction to a more detailed companion sketch to be published in 1991. Whilst not detracting from the completeness of this sketch, it will look more closely at the whole of development into the 90's including the increasing importance of Housing Associations; shared housing; inner area development and renovations; co-operative housing schemes; hostels and warden assisted accommodation together with other Council innovations designed to combat the ever increasing encroachment and restrictions imposed by Central Government. It will also include personal stories of the new generation of Council Tenants and how they see their lives as tenants developing. They will also have the opportunity to reply to the general criticism levelled at them by the earlier generations in this sketch.

Because newspapers are, in themselves a contemporary history of events, the following extracts from the Leicester Mercury and the old Illustrated Leicester Chronicle are presented verbatim. The extracts are by kind permission of the Editor, as are most of the photographs.

"Day by day, the face of Leicester is changing..."

LEICESTER MERCURY
THURSDAY
APRIL 17TH 1952

Nineteen Thousand Houses Booked To Come Down

LEICESTER Development Plan for the next twenty years which is published today, is estimated to involve the expenditure of £100 million in public and private capital, the demolishing of nineteen thousand five hundred and fifty eight houses, and the movement of thousands of people outside the City boundary.

Six main areas are to be cleared and redeveloped as residential areas and the spreading of the City into the surrounding County areas will enable more space to be provided for industry and more for open spaces.

At the same time, steps will be taken to prevent the growth of the City from getting out of hand. There will be no vast sprawl such has occurred in some other industrial areas ... and industrial growth will be controlled.

... On each estate there will be: 'Neighbourhood Planning' with open spaces, allotments, schools, shops, churches and public buildings. Sites are reserved for fourteen Community Centres and eighteen Health Centres.

Main areas due for clearance and redevelopment for residential use are Gresham Street, Wharf Street, Highfields, Charnwood Street, New Parks Street and New Bridge Street ...

ILLUSTRATED
LEICESTER CHRONICLE
MAY 9TH 1953

Our City Expands

LEICESTER is growing up - and out, many of its inhabitants do not know the Leicester of today. To them, the new names to City development areas like Stocking Farm, Eyres Monsell and New Parks are but signboards on Corporation buses.

And what of the City of Tomorrow? To the majority of Leicester people names of future estates such as Scraptoft Valley, Mowmacre, Braunstone Frith and Thurnby Lodge may be as remote as though they were tucked away in the corners of the County.

Huge Modern Estates

It is true to say that the City has grown out of all proportion to its size at the turn of the century. Unlike most of the Cities its growth has come about during comparatively recent times.

Since the last war the huge modern estates at New Parks, Evington and Stocking Farm have been built, accounting for a large part of the eight thousand five hundred and seventy-four houses, shops and prefabs constructed in Leicester during that time. Another vast City and County estate is under construction at Eyres Monsell, South Leicester. There are nearly seven hundred homes occupied there up to date. Between the Hinckley and Groby Roads, Braunstone Frith Estate of four hundred and thirty eight houses has started. For the future, one thousand two hundred and forty houses for City and County will be built at Scraptoft Valley, North of Uppingham Road; One thousand three hundred are planned at nearby Thurnby Lodge; the same number are for the County at Eyres Monsell in addition to those already catered for there; One thousand City homes will be built at Leicester Aerodrome, and seven hundred and sixty new homes will adjoin Stocking Farm estate on what will be called the Mowmacre Project.

LEICESTER MERCURY
SEPTEMBER 3RD 1955

At Hope's Place

I took a stroll around the Wharf Street area yesterday afternoon. What a change is taking place there. The once bustling street where years ago small traders made tidy fortunes, is at a standstill compared with what one can recall.

In other days it had such a glorious mixture of shops, butchers, poulterers, not forgetting the rabbits, general grocers, greengrocers and all the rest with a liberal sprinkling of pubs.

And time was when some people in the sedate parts of Leicester sent to Wharf Street for their best steak and roasting joints, because the butchers there would buy a good beast, but the local trade was all for offal and the cheaper cuts.

In those days the shopkeepers in Wharf Street did more business on Saturday night open until 11 0'clock, and on Sunday morning, than they did throughout the rest of a week.

Desolation

I turned into Eaton Street, half-way along Wharf Street. Under yesterday's evening sun Eaton Street, would have tempted an artist. It should be painted now, sleeping whilst it dies.

Here was a long street of empty houses, windows broken, whole window frames out in places, and doors off their hinges — a crumbling legacy of the piping days of industrial expansion.

They may have grossly overcrowded the ground then, but withal they did not build badly. Just too many houses to the acre.

Guide To Age

Here I found Hope's Place. The name is neatly engraved on a slate tablet over a passage-way leading to a yard and outhouses and what appears to have been a tiny garden, which served the six houses of Hope's Place.

The date on the slate tablet is 1821, and this must be an indication of the age of most of the property at the Wharf Street end of Eaton Street.

One wonders: Who was the Hope who built six houses in Eaton Street just one year after the Mayor and Corporation, accompanied by the High Sheriff had assembled at the High Cross, at Coal Hill and in the Market Place to proclaim George IV King of England — February 3 1820.

It's Quiet Now

In the year Hope's Place was built the town was lit with gas. The population was 30,125.

Now Mr. George Benjamin Mattock is the last occupant of Hope's Place. He's waiting for a bungalow. Where he is he looks out upon the blank staring windows of the houses opposite; upon a street where the grass is now growing between the granite square sets; and from his back door he views a scene of desolation.

But he has lived so long and peacefully in Hope's Place that he does not look forward to the change to a new bungalow in a strange district.

"I'm not a fussy man" he told me "I read my Bible every day and worship at church on Sunday."

Leicester's Wharf Street area immediately after clearance. Taken from the corner of Russell Street and Russell Square; it shows the line of Russell Street. Extreme left is St. Matthews Church and school and on the right Talbot Inn. The dark building in the centre is that of the Wyvern Pen Company Ltd.

LEICESTER MERCURY,
DECEMBER 4, 1957

Day By Day The Face of Leicester is Changing

DAILY Leicester people can see history being made. For amid the roar of the bulldozer and the throb of the cement mixer a new City is emerging.

Everywhere, damp grey slums are being torn from the ground to be replaced with clean modern homes on spacious estates.

Already many drab districts ... have disappeared. Soon work will start on the new St Matthews Estate, to eradicate for all time the cancer that was the old Wharf Street area.

Five Years

Within five years cars will flow along the first stretch of the new ring road ... More dilapidated buildings will crumble in the path of the demolition gang's bulldozer ... Leicester is fast pushing ahead in the speediest development programme in the Midlands to remove blackspots.

Self Sacrifice

Behind much of the work lie countless hours of planning and self sacrifice freely given by a small band of City Councillors.

For the years of planning, discussion and negotiating by the city's Slum Clearance and Redevelopment Committee are bearing fruit.

Over one thousand seven hundred houses have been demolished since 1955. A magnificent total, when it is realised that in Nottingham, a City of comparable size with similar problems, only 131 have been pulled down.

And 15 years hence the last of the nine thousand one hundred houses still on the Slum Clearance Scheme will have been removed. The City's facelift will be complete.

Optimistic Report

Last week the Chairman of the Committee responsible, Alderman C R Keene, gave the City Council an optimistic report of present progress.

Later he explained to the Leicester Mercury that this work was achieved only through immense co-operation with other Committees of the City Council (Planning, Estates and Housing) and the help of the Town Clerk and the Health Department ...

Co-ordination

Alderman Keene said one of the Departments with which his committee had to co-ordinate was the Housing Department. 'We have to be a little bit ahead of them all the time' he commented.

Leicester Mercury,
14th August 1958.

Super Estate

Picture Caption: 'In the slum cleared space near St Matthew's Church, Leicester, a cluster of new buildings is springing up - Leicester's new 'Super Estate' comprising flats and maisonettes. The picture on the right provides an interesting contrast between the old and the new.

13th Sept 1958
A new land-mark now dominates the sky-line in the Lee Street area —
the Wharf Street telephone exchange.

Illustrated Leicester Chronicle,
September 13th, 1958

A NEW LEICESTER IS BORN ...

LEICESTER'S slums come tumbling down ... and out of the rubble a new City is being born.

Now Wharf Street area has a new name - and a new look. Neat, modern flats and maisonettes are going up in three and four storey blocks.

The district is now called St Matthews ... But St Matthews is only one of a dozen places in the City where slum clearance and redevelopments are going on, and where new houses, factories, roads and schools are being built.

Picture Caption: 'This was once Metcalf Street, a dark narrow alley running off Wharf Street. Now, the concrete and steel framework of a block of flats rises where once its cramped and grimy cottages stood ... and this is happening all over the Wharf Street district.

13th Sept 1958
Six weeks ago the demolition gangs arrived in Warrington Street, tucked away between Northgate Street and the Canal. Now most of its tiny four-roomed cottages have been flattened .... to make room for new factories.

Alderman Miss May Goodwin — a dedicated councillor whose first consideration has always been better housing conditions for the people of Leicester.

LEICESTER MERCURY, SEPTEMBER 18TH, 1958

First Tenant Can't See His New Flat

THE door opened yesterday on a new and brighter phase of the life in the old Wharf Street area of Mr J Day. The hand that turned the key in a new flat at 90 Ottawa Road was that of the Lord Mayor, Alderman Sydney Brown.

The only pity is that Mr Day cannot see the fresh compactness of his new four bedroomed home, because he has been blind for 37 of the 60 years he has lived in the area.

But his wife was at his side to tell Mr Day - the first tenant of the first Corporation re-housing project on a slum clearance site - all about the amenities provided in his clean ground floor flat ...

Alderman Miss May Goodwin, Chairman of the Housing Committee, told a Leicester Mercury reporter: 'I am very proud. At one time during the Slum Clearance Scheme I wondered if I should ever live to see it'.

She cited the three and four storey blocks of flats and maisonettes in the new St Matthews Area as an outstanding example of co-operation of all the Council's Committees and Chief Officers and the workmen on the site.

She pointed out that the Housing Committee had now finished its general building programme and all new houses were to rehouse people displaced by the clearance of old property.

The nine thousand houses now left to be pulled down will be tackled at the rate of six hundred a year.

St. Matthews area 3 storey blocks of flats and maisonettes ... "an outstanding example of co-operation ..."

The ground is cleared for the second phase of building on St. Matthews.

August 19th 1959
This three picture composite scene gives a graphic impression of the new vista seen from Wharf Street between Bow Street and Fleet Street.

LEICESTER MERCURY
THURSDAY JULY 6TH,
1961

More Council Homes Will Spring Up Here Next Year

FOLLOWING is a letter written to the Leicester Mercury on the subject of Braunstone Frith.

'Sir - When is something going to be done with the site on the north side of Braunstone Frith School?

'In 1955 a network of concrete roads and drains was laid, presumably for extension to the housing estate but since then this area of some twenty acres has remained derelict, of no further use agriculturally and having no developed use.

'There perhaps was reduction in the number of municipal houses being erected at the time these roads were built, but surely there should have been some signs of building activity during the past five or six years.

'Have the City Authorities completely forgotten about the existence of this site, or do they construct useless roads to get rid of surplus money? John Citizen.

The City Housing Manager reports that this site will come into use next year for a continuation of the estate with more houses, flats and bungalows.

LEICESTER MERCURY

1ST MAY 1970

THIS is the stuff of local Government. This aerial picture of the Civic Trust award winning St Matthews Estate shows through the camera's eye a good cross-section of the material which makes an election address - new roads, new homes, old peoples homes, childrens homes, health centres, industrial development, traffic and schools. It is all there neatly wrapped round by Humberstone Road, Wharf Street and the new perimeter artery, Dysart Way.

Development in the lower part of the picture is St Matthews Phase I completed in 1959; in the upper part St Matthews Phase II completed 1968, the whole comprising flats of various sizes and maisonettes.

Key (A) flatted factory block built to accommodate old businesses displaced by site clearance; (B) Humberstone Road where the shopping centre for the estate is being built; (C) Dysart way linking Humberstone Gate and Belgrave Gate for cross City traffic; (D) Goodwin House and Marston House, the tower blocks of one bedroomed flats; (E) St Matthews Phase I; (F) Wharf Street.

St. Matthews – 'concrete jungle' play area in the early days.

St. Matthews updated — 12 years on.

LEICESTER CHRONICLE,

April 20th, 1973

A Birdseye View ... Stocking Farm

PICTURE Caption: The extremely hilly aspect of Stocking Farm, Leicester, is difficult to imagine from this photograph of the area. Halifax Drive is on the righthand side of the picture, with the hexagonal St Luke's Church to its left. At right angles and in the middle of the picture is Marwood Road.

Rowlatts Hill

October 30th 1984

Two twenty floor skyscraper blocks built on Rowlatts Hill Estate are to date the highest factory-made flats in the Midlands. They contain two hundred and sixty four one bedroomed flats with six flats on each floor.

Fresh air. Nice homes, Freedom — this picture speaks for itself!

Trials and Tribulations
on Netherhall

MRS. Adams lived with her parents in Providence Place, off Hall Street, and except for a fire would no doubt have been there until the slum clearance in the fifties. It was 1947 when they had the fire and the thought of a fire in an area like Providence Place with its back-to-backs; factories; Courts; and a communal entry is frightening! But the family survived the fire and a sympathetic Council housed them in a new home on New Parks Estate.

The family went up on the back of a coal lorry and, ironically, their first priority was to have a fire! Because they had had to move in so quickly, there was no electricity laid on, neither was there provision for heating. But their guardian angel was smiling down upon them because outside there was coke; piles of coke!

As has already been seen the Council seem to have a habit of building houses first and roads after and the coke was to be used as hard core for road laying. The coke would be laid and rolled one day; the next it would be surfaced. As Mrs. Adams said: "Everyone was at it. But the workmen soon twigged that coke was disappearing. After that, they only laid as much as could be surfaced in the day. Still it got us out of the cold!"

Six years, a marriage and two children later, Mrs Adams moved into her present house on Netherhall Road. When she and the family moved in it was February and snowing.

Typically, again, the road wasn't made up and when the furniture arrived the removal men got stuck in the sludge. "I suppose it was very funny really" said Mrs Adams with a laugh. "There were two men with my wardrobe between them, slowly sinking. Eventually workmen got them out, together with my wardrobe which was still intact". She continued: "When we were settled in

TOP: Mrs Adams

BOTTOM: Her home today

98

we kept finding feathers. Eventually we found out that they were the feathers from stolen chickens. Apparently the workmen had been using our house as a lodging; stealing chickens from the field opposite; plucking them and then cooking them for their supper in what was to be our bedroom".

After a few days Mrs. Adams' father - who had worked on similar houses - came to visit them. He took one look at the fireplace; caught hold of the surround and pulled. It came completely away with the two large nails that had been holding it in place!

One day in the kitchen, Mrs. Adams noticed a piece of thread hanging from the tap. "I got hold of it and pulled, and pulled and pulled and suddenly whoosh! water everywhere. I screamed, and old Albert who was just knocking off, came running in to help. That's what they used for washers - string!"

Eventually the family settled in and thought their troubles were over. It was still muddy outside and the road and pavements were not completed. But the house was tidy and Mr. Adams started on the garden. His first priority was a lawn but he needed a firm base.

Outside the workmen had been using tons of clinker to lay foundations for the road, so Mr. Adams saw the foreman and asked if he could have some. "Yes" said the foreman "help yourself. Use the spade and wheelbarrow" So, with alacrity, Mr. Adams set to. Mrs. Adams continued: "He worked like a Trojan - that was until the law turned up in the form of a hefty copper. 'Where are you going with that then?' 'I'm laying a lawn. I've got the O.K from the foreman'

Lang's "Easi-form" houses being built in 1946

'Take it back - take all of it back, go on!' And so he did. But do you know, years later, there were still mounds of grass-covered clinker opposite! And they would have been there now if the Tenants' Association hadn't got them moved.

"But all that was a long time ago. We would like to buy the house ourselves now but we looked at mortgage costs and knew we wouldn't be able to cope. Still, it's not too bad, the children have all grown up and we've got good neighbours - in fact with the exception of a couple of houses we're all 'originals' in this block.

Speaking of children, you hear all sorts of things about kids on Council Estates, but in this block there were twenty seven and they all turned out O.K. You see those trees over there, they were put in as saplings and not one was broken or pulled out. Would it be the same with 1989?"

As I drove away from Mrs. Adams, something hit the car. I got out and a young lad was picking up a frisbee. I looked at the car and then at him. He could've run away. But he didn't. He came up: "Sorry, I didn't mean it, it was an accident" "That's O.K" I said, "No damage. Thanks for apologising".

There's a moral there somewhere.

From Asylum Street
to the Asylum and Central Heating installed within a month

BERTIE Dunkley, was born sixty nine years ago in Asylum Street at the back of the Leicester Royal Infirmary and was christened at St Andrews Church. Recently, he had occasion to go to the 'Royal' and with time to spare looked up his old haunts.

The home he was born in had disappeared; the only landmark for its whereabouts being the pub at the corner. According to Mr. Dunkley, the pub hadn't changed at all except for a facelift. As he looked towards the Swan and Rushes, his memories came flooding back. "I remember that behind the Swan and Rushes, there was an alleyway which led to the bakers where, because there was no real cooking facilities in our pokey old houses, we used to take the Sunday dinner to be cooked. Charabanc rides in what was like a boat on wheels; a school that was no longer there, and, in 1925, the Big Blaze when a shoe factory went up like a rocket!"

In 1925, Bertie's father was offered a Council house on Tailby Estate. Because his father had fought in the war, the house was truly one 'fit for heroes'.

"The house backed on to the Asylum (now The Towers) in Humberstone Lane and, after the terraces of Asylum Street, the view was wonderful. At the bottom of the garden was some trees and shrubbery; beyond, railings, a wide drive and more railings; then, lovely fields. And, as a backdrop, the red brick buildings of the Towers. Even the rent collector used to comment on the view," recalls Bertie. "He always said: 'The view from the bottom of your garden is wonderful, isn't it. You should be paying at least a quid for a view like that'.

"Altogether, the family lived there for forty six years until mother died. Initially, there were eight of us - my mother, father, my uncle, my brother and three sisters and myself. And the house was just right for us all.

"Before Tailby School was built I went to Harrison Road. To get there, we had to catch two buses. I always remember one of the drivers, we called him 'Walrus' because he had a very big moustache. It was whilst I was at Harrison Road that I had a series of illnesses but they didn't really hold me back. And it was during one of them that I watched Tailby Estate School being built. It was a wooden prefab type building, and I watched them daily as they put it together.

> *"You should be paying at least a quid for a view like that..."*

> *"The area where we live is so nice..."*

Little did I realise then, that that was going to be the school in which I was going to end my school days. Now, of course, it is Mundella School and the buildings are extensive and in brick.

"I also watched Northfields Estate being built. Before it was built, there were lots of cattle in the fields belonging to the farm and I remember once they had foot and mouth disease. Even now, I can see the cattle quite clearly, legs in the air being burned to get rid of the disease. Sometimes, I used to go across the fields to Scraptoft Golf Links and earn myself a bob or two caddying. One of the things I'll never forget is going to Brighton Road Mission. I think it's a Community Centre now but we used to go every Sunday without fail. I notice that today, no-one seems to bother to go to those sort of places anymore. But on Tailby in my day we all did. Money used to go a long way for us kids too. I remember in 1935 I had sixpence and I walked down Victoria Road East to the Cinema. On the way was a chocolate shop called Pratts. I went in and bought a bar of chocolate and a packet of Crown cigarattes; I got two cigarettes and two matches. Then I went to the Shaftesbury Cinema. On the way back I had to pass a fish and chip shop and I went in there for a penny worth of chips and scratchings. In the

quarter of a mile to where I lived, I'd eaten my chips and scratchings and reckon that for five pence, with a penny change, I'd had a damn good night out.

"Time went on and eventually I got married. My wife and I lived in Brazil Street to begin with and after a few months, we were lucky enough to get a flat on East Park Road. This was very nice and quite large, but when our daughter came along we decided it was time that we, too, applied for a Council house. And so we got ourselves a house at Netherhall, on Keyham Lane West. That was in 1952 and we stayed there for two years. Opposite to us were fields and it was very dark. There were not many lights, and if you looked out of the back window at Selby Avenue all was pitch black. And my wife didn't like it. So she said, 'If we get a chance to move, Bert, I think we should'. That was thirty two years ago and in 1957 we moved to our present house. The Council have been very good to us. About five years ago my wife, having developed an infirmity, wanted us to move to a bungalow. But the area where we live is so nice, that I said no. The Council then provided me with a stairlift so my wife could get up the stairs - smashing".

Mr. Dunkley then spoke of the advantage of only having to go to an area office when before he had to go to New Walk Centre.

"Yes, it's good. It's not far from the Health Centre on Uppingham Road, so when I park my car on the Health Centre car park, all I have to do is go across the road. It's quite handy also on Netherhall Road. There is a

Council House Snips

rent office there which is quite easy to get to and I have no complaints whatsoever. You often hear people complaining about repairs and so on. But I don't know whether I'm lucky, but if I want anything doing it is done within a matter of days or at most a week or two. Take, for example when we put in for central heating. We applied for it in January, and by February (4 weeks later) it was installed. Only recently, I was telling the people in Uppingham Road Office how great it was. The morning that they came along to install the central heating was a brilliant beautiful day. But by 11 o'Clock it had started to snow so, my wife and I went along to Age Concern. We came home in the afternoon and the snow must have been at least six inches deep. The workmen were still there and they were still working and one of them said 'We've got your central heating going'. And I said 'Yes, but it's 4 o'clock, you usually go by 4'. They said 'Yes we know, but you feel the radiators' and, sure enough, they were warm, and by 5 o'clock, everything was finished. You can't really complain about service like that, can you?"

Sitting in his cosy front room with a barrel of home brew on the side - "I check it every day so I know precisely when I've got to do my next lot" - Bertie and his wife reflected on their council house life. Finally Bertie said, "Do you know, it must say something for Council house life because in the thirty eight years we've been here, I don't remember my wife or myself ever having a wry word!"

STRIKE A LIGHT!

WHEN the War broke out and we had to blackout, I said to my mum: 'We'll have to put some blackout curtains at the back'. 'No we won't' said mother, 'We'll just lock the gate, then the air raid warden won't be able to get round to see!'"

BIRTHS, MARRIAGES AND DEATHS JOB

WHEN we lived in our two-up two-down, we did everything in the back room. We never used the front, it was always kept spick and span. Piano. Chairs. Pictures on the walls - everything was regularly cleaned. But nobody died while we were there!

HARD LABOUR

WHEN we moved in, the ground at the back was all bricks, broken pipes, lumps of concrete; twitch like a carpet and sub-soil right to the top of the fence. But, we dug a big hole and buried the twitch in it. Then we levelled the ground and double dug it. Then the Council came along just to make sure we were keeping the garden up to scratch!"

Council house gardens kept 'up to scratch'!

Glovers Walk shows how far council planning has progressed in 70 years: the sort of planning that has received accolades from Europe.

Leicester does it once again

IF Braunstone in the '20s' and St. Matthews in the '50s' were developments that caught the imagination of council estate developers, then Beaumont Leys in the '70s', was not only to bring praise from the Department of the Environment, but also accolades from Europe. In fact, Scandinavia was destined to send local authority representatives to see at first hand what could be done; to applaud the exercise, and go home with new ideas - praise, indeed, from a country in the forefront of European housing and estate design.

But when one looks at the name, Beaumont Leys, perhaps it is only right and proper that it should receive an accolade from Europe, for the name is probably derived from tbe French meaning 'Beautiful Hill'.

Beaumont Leys goes back in time to the days of William the Conqueror, when the estate was given to Hugh de Grentemesnil as a reward for his support of William.

From before 1168, the land was in the hands of the Beaumont family. The Cinquefoil, the five leaved emblem of the city arms, can be attributed to Robert Fitz-Pernell (de Beaumont) who died in 1206.

On a political basis, Beaumont Leys has yet another claim to fame. Simon De Montfort, the Earl of Leicester who formed England's first parliament, sold part of Beaumont Leys to the Knights Hospitallers, one of the great monastic orders of knighthood. Eventually the Hospitallers exchanged their land with the Duchy of Lancaster in 1482. Soon afterwards, Edward IV designated Beaumont Leys as a Royal deer park. But enough of history, to get back to the planning of Beaumont Leys.

Conceived as a satellite town to house some 40,000 people, Beaumont Leys was to be completely self-contained - a happy mix

"Conceived as a Satellite town to house some 40,000 people, Beaumont Leys was to be completely self-contained..."

9th December 1975. The official ceremony to hand over the keys to the first tenants moving in on the new Beaumont Leys estate.

Early days of the Beaumont Leys development – this aerial view shows Anstey Lane and the Severn-Trent buildings in the foreground

106

of industry, commerce, private and council housing, the whole to blend happily together, with wide roads, landscaping, and open spaces being the order of the day. In planning, contours and the countryside had been taken into consideration to ensure that Beaumont Leys did not intrude upon the green and pleasant land. Building was to be controlled by the Council, thereby preventing private development getting out of control. And so it was that, in 1974, with link roads designed to connect with both the City and the motorway, work on both industrial and housing sites began.

With a potential local workforce and excellent communications, Beaumont Leys was a 'natural' for the industrialist, and options were quickly taken up. On Gorse Hill, Artisan Press took a site of 6 acres,

whilst on Bursom Industrial Park, Walkers Crisps built their 130,000 sq.ft. factory on a 7 acre site. Other companies both large and small took out options and, today, work harmoniously side by side in custom built sections.

Whilst the industrial sites were being developed, work began on private and council housing. Astill Lodge and Heatherbrook were soon a healthy mix of council and private houses ranging from semis, through disabled persons bungalows and warden assisted units, to detached houses — all beautifully landscaped. As time went on, housing continued on Castle Hill, Keepers Lodge West, Beaumont Park, Glebelands and Glebe Lodge.

Beaumont Leys now has four primary schools, a community college, neighbourhood centres at Barleycroft, Home Farm, and Beaumont Lodge. At Beaumont Lodge, a youth wing has recently been added. Medically, the residents have a health centre and two doctors' surgeries and, as the estate continues to develop, more will no doubt be added.

A main feature of the estate is the Leisure Centre. This was opened in 1985 as a complex offering fun and games for everyone. The main feature is the mixture of pools. The Pool Hall has a main pool which drops in stages to 6½ feet at its deepest point; a leisure pool with an overall depth of 3½ feet for toddlers; a dimple pool for babies and the flume pool. The flume gives an exciting ride - over 100 feet of water assisted slide with curves and tunnels - the first to be installed in Leicester. Behind the leisure pool are three chambers which, with compressed air, create waves up to 3 feet high.

The Sports Hall is equipped for most games. It has 5 cricket tunnels and a fitness area and can be used for spectator sports. For mothers with young children a creche

A similar view just a few years later in 1981 – the estate has grown and new roads have been opened up

A corner of the
Beaumont
Shopping Centre
which became
the subject of
media
speculation in
1975

108

is provided. Like any other leisure centre, Leicester Leys would not be complete without its bars and facilities for dancing; live bands; discos; barbeques and even fashion shows. The hall is also available for birthday, anniversary, and wedding celebrations.

The leisure centre is on a 1 acre site set in 55 acres of parkland. The entire park will shortly be landscaped to blend like the rest of Beaumont Leys, harmoniously with the surrounding countryside.

No introduction to Beaumont Leys would be complete without mentioning the Ecumenical Church. This is the Church Centre of Christ the King and is Leicester's first ecumenical centre. Here, 5 denominations share their faith - Baptists, Congregational, Methodist, Church of England and the United Reform Church.

In 1986 Leicester City Council commissioned a series of 6 whole page articles in the Leicester Mercury on the development of Beaumont Leys and to extol its virtues.

This was a public relations exercise designed to allay disquiet among certain residents over adverse media coverage. The articles were well received and in response to requests by both regular residents and newcomers, they were reproduced in edited form, in a booklet which was to be given to all new residents.

By early 1975, the first Council tenants had moved in and almost immediately, what appeared to be a second North Braunstone situation developed. Whether it was the 'bored youth' syndrome of the 70s, just adverse media comments or something entirely different, is something on which one should not speculate. Therefore, because - as in the case of North Braunstone - Beaumont Leys seems to make the headlines with a monotonous regularity, this is something which it is hoped can be explored in the companion sketch in consultation with Ward Councillors, tenants and the younger generation. But suffice it to say, that as early as August 1975, the media were already making waves even though the estate was as yet undeveloped, by comparing it to Liverpool's Kirby New Town with such comments as: "Packs of youths are already wandering aimlessly around the estate... Later on, when a shopping centre is built, residents fear it will act as a magnet for bored youngsters."

This is the first mention of the Beaumont Shopping Centre and it has been left until this point in the story so that comparison may be made with the media speculations of 1975. Beaumont Shopping Centre is visited by people from all over the city, and all agree that with its variety of shops; its outdoor market; local pub; large car parks and the nearby leisure centre, it is a lovely place. And they prove this by coming back again and again.

On the social side, Beaumont Leys has a community newspaper which, in it's 'What's On' column quotes on average some 100 activities ranging from playgroups for toddlers to a variety of youth activities; and from sport, to old time dancing and senior citizens' clubs. There is swimming and popmobility; and there's aquarist and micro-clubs. And the unemployed aren't forgotten either, for there is always a drop-in night for them at one of the neighbourhood centres.

The senior citizens' groups are particularly successful with attendances of over 100 at a time at their social events.

By April 1989, a total of 2,269 housing units had been built. These comprised 1, 2 and 3 bedroomed flats, 2, 3, 4 and 5 bedroomed houses, 1 bedroomed bungalows, 3 bedroomed bungalows and 3 bedroomed maisonettes.

To conclude this chapter, let us go back to the Beaumont Leys booklet and quote from it:

"... it (Beaumont Leys) is only the beginning of a success story that will be marvelled at a hundred years from now.

"Future generations in Leicester will view a suburb set amid trees, greensward and flowers, in which privately owned and council built homes have their place; where discreetly sited light industry offers employment, and a large shopping centre and strategically placed single shops serve the needs of the area."

1976 saw the opening ceremony for new council houses and bungalows for disabled people on the estate

The Housing Bill –
Tenants act and Leicester City Council makes history

The Times, November 11, 1988

'GUILLOTINE ENDS MARATHON HOUSING BILL

ESPITE bitter protests from opposition MP's, the Housing Bill completed its passage through the Commons after the Government had carried a timetable motion curtailing debate on it.

The Bill provides for the establishment of Housing Action Trusts, which are intended to take over run-down housing estates and to improve them...

The Guillotine Motion was carried by 303 votes to 176 - Government majority, 127".

Thus ended a struggle involving Central Government and all opposition parties, and last but certainly not least, Tenants' Associations.

Mention has already been made in earlier chapters of the origin and activities of Tenants' Associations during the early days of the estates; the way they sought action from the Council in anything that affected tenants; how they developed socially and fostered the Community spirit.

Since those early days, Tenants' Associations have organised themselves both locally and nationally, through the Federation of Tenants' Association. This is a national body with local branches to which Tenants' Associations are affiliated. The branches co-ordinate and represent Tenants' Associations both locally and nationally, thus enabling them to make an impact on provincial and national matters.

An essential requirement of Tenants' Associations is that they present a non-political front, for therein lies their strength; the knowledge that they can negotiate impartially and work closely with a Council and its officers - whatever the political colour, without fear or favour. Associations have their own offices on the estates where tenants can drop in to discuss individual problems, and where regular meetings for tenants to discuss all estate business are organised. The organisation is through Tiers. These are:

Tier 3: Grass Roots. Monthly meetings with individual Associations.

Tier 2: Intermediate level. Regular meetings with Area Housing Staff and Ward Councillors, attended by two officers from each Tenants' Association within the area.

Tier 1: Top level. Meetings on matters of City-wide importance and urgency with Housing Committee Chairman, top Council officials and representatives of all city Tenants' Associations.

An excellent example of how Tenants' Associations in conjunction with Councils, can influence a national issue started in 1986 when Central Government presented its Housing and Planning Bill. The main thrust of the Bill was recommendations for the privatisation of Council estates.

It all started innocuously enough - as most Government legislation does, but within a few short months of ever increasing debate, it was obvious that the Bill was due for a very rough passage indeed.

The Bill affected many areas of housing, including:

★ an extension of the 'Right to Buy' legislation, the incentive being an increased discount.

★ allow the Secretary of State to sell off complete estates to private landlords (Housing Action Trusts).

★ to give local Housing Authorities powers to sell off estates — with the approval of the Secretary of State — to private companies and approved landlords, the Secretary to have the power to provide grants to the new management.

★ to give private landlords the chance to increase rents and reduce the tenants' security of tenure.

When the proposed Bill was examined, particularly in relation to previous Government restrictions on Council house spending and the reduction on Housing Grants, reaction from Local Government was predictable; a predictability endorsed by the Tenants' Associations, particularly when the wide ranging powers given to councils to sell off whole estates was fully realised. Both saw the Bill as the beginning of the end of Council estates - and Council house

people. The pioneering work at the turn of the century; development between the wars and the innovations of postwar development - all this was now, it seemed, to be put on the slippery slope to Council house oblivion.

As the Housing Bill butted its way through the ever mounting seas of parliamentary debate, so did media coverage. The build up started from small beginnings. In a '12cm single column', the Sunday Express started:

"COUNCILS MAY LOSE HOUSING

SHOCK plans to remove 4½ million Council houses from Local Authority Control were unveiled yesterday.

"Housing Minister John Patten said he wants the entire stock sold off or handed over to Housing and Tenants' Associations or private institutions ... This will be accompanied by legislation to pave the way for a major boost to privately rented houses and flats.

"The Government wants to see more rented accommodation available for young single people, newly married couples and the elderly".

Local TAs preparing to march to demonstrate their opposition to the Bill.

111

Close on its heels came a further report, this time in The Telegraph and running into two columns.

'PATTEN'S COUNCIL HOUSING IDEA 'WILL HIT THE HOMELESS'

SUGGESTIONS by Mr Patten, the Housing Minister, that the Government might break up large Council housing estates by limiting the number of properties which local authorities can own was described yesterday as a 'substitute for a real housing policy'.

"Mr Edward Cantle, Under-Secretary responsible for Housing at the Association of Metropolitan Authorities, said the proposal would make it more difficult for councils to carry out their duties towards the homeless.

His criticsm was echoed by Mr Sam Darby, Chairman of Manchester City Council's Housing Committee, who said: 'This kind of suggestion from John Patten is typical of his ill informed approach to Council Housing'.

"Mr Patten's thinking on future Government Policy indicated that one long-term aim would be the ending of the role of Councils as landlords.

"A first step within the next five to ten years would be an upper limit on Council-owned housing, with Building Societies, Pension Funds, Housing Associations and Tenants' Co-operatives filling the gap left by Local Authorities.

"Mr Simon Hughes, the Liberal Housing spokesman said yesterday: 'We deplore the appalling privatisation dogma of the Tories. Council housing has its problems, but it remains the corner stone of provision for Britain's homeless and badly housed."

"A spokesman for Mr Patten last night denied that the Minister intended to eliminate Councils as landlords. It was merely intended to reduce the size of their holdings..."

As the debate hotted up Councils were being asked for guidelines from anxious tenants. Not surprisingly, many were concerned and the Tenants' Associations began to take action. But let Mrs. Kath Stevens, an Officer of Stocking Farm and Abbey Rise Tenants' Association tell what happened. I asked Mrs. Stevens to tell me about tenants' first reactions to the proposed Bill, their feelings and fears.

"Well, we had lots of people come to the tenants' office full of fears. They were convinced that private landlords would take them over, and put the prices up so high that they wouldn't be able to afford the payments and that they would be turned out. And I suppose this reaction was natural because some of them had been living in their houses for 20 and 30 years. However, the first thing we did was to try and put their fears at rest by telling them that the Bill wasn't Law yet. But you can understand the fear because nothing like this had happened to them before.

"Time went on and tenants began to lose interest, thinking nothing would ever happen. But then, the debate became personal to Leicester with local MP's

debating through the local press. This stirred up fears once again and, finally, the City Council Housing Chair agreed to join our delegation of tenants to the House of Commons to lobby our local MP's. We wanted to tell them that, as tenants, we didn't want our homes taken over but wanted to stay with the Council.

"And in organising the delegation, we were not alone. Twenty other Local Authorities were doing the same."

In Leicester, more than 5,000 signatures against the sale of estates was collected and, against a background of debates on local radio between conflicting Councillors and a general hotting up of the debate in all local media, the delegation departed for London.

February 11th 1987 dawned grey and misty, but that didn't dampen the spirits of the tenants' delegation and, by 2.30pm, they were in the House. But, Mrs. Stevens recalled, "We were not very favourably received. We were simply trying to put across to them that we didn't want private landlords to take over Council homes, as no more were being built because the Government had cut the Housing Grant. And if any were sold, other than those sold to Council tenants, the actual stock left to house people who could not afford to buy, would get less and less until eventually there would be none at all. But then, the MP for Leicester West arrived; calmed everyone down and put our case.

"The thing that was really worrying us was the fact that under the proposals, those tenants who didn't vote would be counted as a 'yes' vote, as would houses that were not even occupied. Therefore, if only a minority actually voted 'yes', that minority could then be turned quite easily into majority by adding the non voters as 'yes' votes. So, whichever way you look at it, it wasn't going to be a fair vote at all. However, when our visit was all over, we came away feeling that at least as a Tenants' Association, we had tried, and we hoped that some good would come out of the visit. All we could do now would be to go back and if ever a situation arose where the Council was going to sell off an estate, then we would have to do all we could to ensure that *every* tenant voted so that the vote would be a fair one.

"But we in Leicester are very fortunate, because the Council has assured us that they will not sell off any estates unless they are really forced and it was really as a result of these talks that the Charter was conceived".

After the House of Commons visit, the Federation kept up the pressure, obtaining excellent news coverage for its activities. One, in particular, was a public meeting at which Langburgh Council tenants from Cleveland, supported by Shelter, Manchester, were to speak out again against the selling-off of Council Estates and talk about their year-long struggle to stay in their Council houses. The meeting was held in Southfields Library and such was media interest, that it was filmed by Central TV for 'Central Lobby.'

But time was running out. And on the day after the guillotining, November 12th, all the fears that had been expressed by Tenants' Associations and others were confirmed:

In The Independent:
'COUNCIL TO SELL HOMES DESPITE BALLOT

A CONSERVATIVE-controlled Council is to press ahead with the £56m sale of its entire housing stock to two Housing Associations, despite an overwhelming vote against the transfer by the majority of tenants who voted.

"The ballot of Torbay Council tenants was the first test of the Government's decision to count those who failed to take part in ballots under the new Housing Bill as voting 'yes'. The 5,200 tenants voted three to one against the sale, with nearly 60% of them turning out to vote.

"But under the rules governing such transfers, those who do not vote can be counted as being in favour as will also be the case in ballots of Council tenants who 'opt out' under the Housing Bill when it becomes law. On this basis the Torbay figures show 58% for the transfer of the estate. Tony Key, the Council Leader, said the wide publicity for the system of voting meant that 'Many of those in favour of the sell off simply did not bother to vote'.

"But Darren Cowell of Torbay Labour Party, which has campaigned against the transfer, described the voting process as undemocratic. He hoped that all parties would abandon the idea.

"He said the Council's refusal to supply a list of tenants to those opposing the transfer had made it very difficult for them to ensure the absolute defeat of the proposal. 'It meant we were stabbing in the dark - yet as it was we only lost it by about 400 votes'.

"Local Authorities have had the power to make large scale transferring of Council houses since 1985 though none have yet taken place because the detailed rules governing them were not published until earlier this year".

The Daily Mirror put it more succinctly:

"ANGER AT SELL OFF

ALL the homes owned by a Council are to be sold - despite a three to one vote against by tenants. The £56m sale will make the Council at Torbay, Devon, the first to sell its entire stock of houses. The sale is going ahead because under new Government rules, anyone not voting counts as a yes vote.

Angry Labour Party Area Secretary Darren Cowell said 'This is a most undemocratic voting process'".

Likewise with The Guardian:

"COUNCIL TO SELL HOMES IN SPITE OF MINORITY VOTE

THE homes of 5,200 Council tenants are to be sold off although only 787 of them - a clear minority - backed the transfer in Britain's first 'tenant's choice' ballot. The result was declared yesterday."

But for Torbay tenants, all was not lost.

Perhaps the comments of Kate Stevens when she said that she hoped some good would come out of the visit to the Commons are pertinent here. Or, perhaps it was the violent reactions of all opposing political parties to the voting anomaly of the Bill. Who knows? But whatever it was, it worked. The estates were not sold off. For when it came to the crunch, Nicholas Ridley vetoed the sale!

"... at least we had tried, and we hoped that some good would come out of the visit."

115

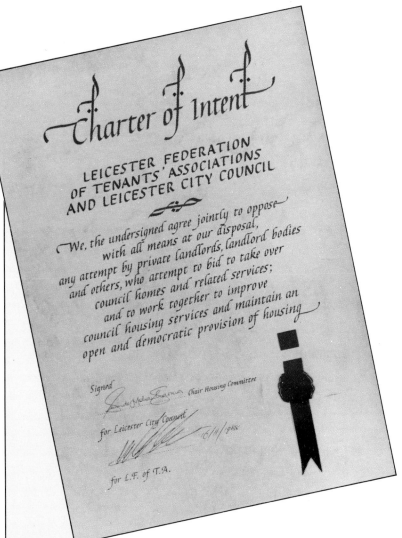

CHARTER OF INTENT
Leicester Federation of Tenants' Associations and Leicester City Council

"We, the undersigned agree jointly to oppose, with all means at our disposal, any attempt by private landlords, landlord bodies and others, who attempt to bid to take over Council homes and related services; and to work together to improve Council housing services and maintain an open and democratic position of housing."

Signed by the Chair of the Housing Committee on behalf of Leicester City Council and the General Secretary of the Leicester Federation of Tenants Associations on behalf of the tenants, the Charter is now an historic document in Leicester City Council's Housing history, representing as it does, a partnership of Council and Tenants united in a common cause.

The Charter of Intent between the City Council and the Leicester Federation of Tenants' Associations, signed in 1988

On Wednesday November 16th 1988, several hundred people gathered in the magnificent 19th century Ballroom in Leicester's City Rooms to witness the signing of the Charter, and to hear representatives of Leicester City Council, Leicester Federation of Tenants' Associations and the Social Housing Consortium explain their future actions now that the Housing Bill had received the royal assent.

The Meeting was chaired by Councillor Surinder Sharma, Chair of Leicester City Council's Housing Committee, supported by Ted Cantle, Director of Housing, Leicester City Council, and the General Secretary of the Leicester Federation of Tenants' Associations. In the presence of the City's Labour MP's and supportive Councillors, Ted Cantle opened the meeting where he laid on the line the City Council's and the Federations' intentions. These were added to by Councillor Surinder Sharma and Keith Vaz Labour MP, Leicester East. After the declarations, Surinder Sharma read out the Charter and duly signed it together with the General Secretary of the Federation of Tenants Associations.

Afterwards, Kate Squire-Taylor of BBC Radio Leicester interviewed the three principals together with two groups of tenants and her broadcast is printed verbatim:

'A Charter of Intent between Leicester City Council and the City Tenants' Association Federation. City Council Director of Housing Ted Cantle explains:

"What we are jointly agreeing to do is to oppose any bids by private landlords or other bodies, property speculators, or whoever want to take over Council estates. We have also agreed that we are going to work together to get a better service for our tenants so that tenants want to stay with us. There are a good number of Tenants Associations here. We have got about 46 all together and I think all of them unanimously have said that they don't want the Bill. They find that the voting procedure is unacceptable and that they want to stay as part of the City Council and be in a genuine partnership for better service."

Every Council tenant will have the right to vote but it is being operated on what is being called a 'negative' vote system, Ted Cantle again:

"What the Government are proposing to do is to count everybody who doesn't vote as a vote in favour of a new landlord. That means, that on an estate of say 100 properties, if 1 tenant votes for a new landlord and 49 vote for the Council, the estate is nevertheless transferred because the 50 who didn't vote are all counted as voting for the new landlord. So just 1 tenant carries the majority of 49 tenants".

The Government believes it will give tenants greater choice by expanding the private rented sector and reducing the role of local Councils as landlords. But all 3 Labour MP's in the City of Leicester are against it and support the Charter, Keith Vaz the MP for Leicester East:

"I agree with freedom of choice but if they are going to give powers to people to choose their landlords, why don't they give people in private rented accommodation the right to opt out of private rented accommodation and from local authority control? They are not giving that choice to those people, they are being absolutely selective".

Chairman of the Housing Committee Surinder Sharma says the operation of the new law will be complicated, but if a tenant votes NO, they will have a statutory right to stay in their homes, he says the Bill doesn't address the real problems in housing:

TOP: Councillor Sheila Mitchell (Liberal Democrat) addresses the meeting

BOTTOM: Members of the audience in the City Rooms listen intently as the issues are discussed

HOUSING ACT
DON'T PANIC!
"This Act does not
affect warden
assisted or elderly
peoples' accommodation"

HOUSING ACT
"A local housing
service from
your local
landlord"

HC
"You
right
Coun
BUT YOU

TOP:
*Councillor Jack
Allan puts the
Conservative
point of view
from an all party
panel including
local MPs, Jim
Marshall and
Keith Vaz*

BOTTOM:
*A tenant makes
his point*

118

"The Housing Bill doesn't address homelessness, it doesn't address the building of new Council homes, it doesn't address the problem of Councils facing restrictions on capital expenditure. All it says is that existing stock that Council's have, may be transferred over to private landlords. So the Government doesn't actually address the major housing issues, the underspending on capital expenditure on Council estates, the long waiting lists. We've got ten thousand people on our waiting list, we've got six thousand people on our transfer list and more and more people becoming homeless who we can't house".

But surely they would argue that by expanding the rented sector those waiting lists will decrease through a market economy?

"They are not expanding the rented sector, the Council estates are the rented sector, they're just transferring it from one landlord, or trying to, to another one".

I spoke to tenants from New Parks Association and asked them what they felt about the Bill.

"There are a lot of worried people in this City, I can assure you".

Do you not think it's going to give you more choice though?

"No, not at our time of life anyway. This is the point, and the thing is you see, should they put the rents up, a lot of people are going to be out of their home, so it's going to be thousands of us wandering about all over the place".

"I have been a Council tenant since 1938. Before that I was under a private landlord and he was a very excellent person as far as charities were concerned, but he wasn't a good landlord, and I know very well that we shall be worse off, far worse off".

And so, for Leicester at least, the die is now cast. And whatever the political rights or wrongs of the Act, it's not for this sketch to judge. But Leicester Tenants' Associations are clear about the road they wish to follow for the foreseeable future in relation to privatisation of their estates.

Epilogue 1990

SITTING in his favourite chair, replete after an excellent meal, Fred, now with a grown up family and grandchildren of his own, picked up a book on housing reform and began to read. Soon his thoughts, stimulated by the book, began to wander, and he found himself reflecting on his forebears' history; how so much of it was mirrored in the book he was reading. He thought of Jimmy and the stinking courts of the 19th Century. What would he think if he came back today. For sure, he wouldn't believe the truth of his eyes. He would see his great great grandchildren, their children and their children's children living in homes ranging from cosy council semis, through detached houses to a country lodge. And in the main, he would find them happy and healthy. But Fred wonders how different the situation would have been if the Corporations of 1835 and 1919 had not acted as they did; and if the heritage they had created, had not been carried on by the Councils of today.

In the field of council housing, much is happening and will happen in the 1990's - a lot of it not for the better. But at least, today's Council House People know that with the Tenants' Charter as proof of the City Council's sincerity, and a Housing Department dedicated to carry out its aims, their council house future will not be failed for want of dedication to a cause.

Fred felt tired and drifted into a doze. But before he fell asleep he thought about his grandchildren's future. He could see them now, sitting in their push-button homes reviewing the 20th Century. Would they look back with pride? envy? pity?

But supposing the houses were not push-button; supposing they were ... Fred was asleep.

Author's note. I cannot verify the Preface, the story having been passed on by successive generations by word of mouth. But the remainder, yes. Tom and Elizabeth Merry were my grandparents.

F.W.W.

Acknowledgments

To name every individual and every company
who helped to make this sketch possible
could run to several pages.
Therefore, to everyone who in any way
contributed to it's success, to all of you,
my most grateful thanks. Bill.

Bibliography

"From Slums to Semis"	Ned Newitt
"Housing and Town Planning in Leicester"	Cllr. H.W. Hallam, J.P.
"Leicester Past and Present"	Jack Simmons
"Leicester, the Making of a Modern City"	Robert Guy Waddington
"Victoria County History of Leicester"	Ed. Dr. W.G. Hoskins
"Victorian Houses"	David Rubinstein

Leicester City Council : Housing Department Archives
Planning Department Archives
Council Minutes and Records